ADVANCE PRAISE

"Bob has already brought the benefit of applying his JTBD principles to two of the three most important areas in business: product strategy and marketing. This book tackles the third and arguably the most important: sales. Most sales gurus obsess about how to sell. Bob instead invests his time in the more important and underserved side of the equation: how people buy. The result is a fresh perspective and new ideas for an age-old trade."

—DES TRAYNOR, CO-FOUNDER AND CHIEF
STRATEGY OFFICER, INTERCOM

"I have always enjoyed my interactions with Bob Moesta, as do our demanding students. His work with regard to JTBD is top shelf. I am so glad he is now taking his creative engineering mindset to sales with his new book "Demand-Side Sales 101." Sales is the lifeblood of any organization and unfortunately, it is too often seen as black magic. We need a more systematic way to approach sales and this extension of JTBD to sales fills an important gap. I recommend this book to anyone in business because nothing really happens until there is a sale."

—BILL AULET, PROFESSOR, MIT SLOAN; MANAGING
DIRECTOR OF THE MARTIN TRUST CENTER
FOR MIT ENTREPRENEURSHIP, AND AUTHOR
OF *DISCIPLINED ENTREPRENEURSHIP*

"Bob applies his engineering mindset to the sales process. His unique perspective puts a new spin on sales that shows the reader how to sell from the buyer's perspective. What results is a thoughtful and comprehensive book that equips you to look at sales through a different lens, with frameworks that make it easy to apply the theory."

—JOHN ROSELLI, GENERAL MANAGER, BOSE HEALTH

"Bob continues to innovate and apply JTBD principles to many aspects of a business. Sales are one place where it is desperately needed. His empathetic perspective and diverse background bring a fresh perspective to an age-old—and critical—set of skills and disciplines. Most impressively, Bob has applied his engineering thinking to create a process that mirrors how people buy, not how we want to sell. Progress should be the new mantra for sales."

—CRAIG WORTMANN, CLINICAL PROFESSOR OF ENTREPRENEURSHIP, KELLOGG SCHOOL OF MANAGEMENT AT NORTHWESTERN UNIVERSITY; FOUNDER AND EXECUTIVE DIRECTOR OF THE KELLOGG SALES INSTITUTE; CEO, SALES ENGINE, INC.

"I recently took on the role of leading marketing and needed a resource that helped me cut through all of the marketing buzzwords and fads. My company is counting on me for results, not vanity metrics. This book has enabled me to truly understand how best to engage with prospects at each stage of their decision. We have moved away from pushing features at prospects to engaging them in conversations that offer benefits on their terms. As a result, our sales team has prospects who are ready to make qualified decisions, *and our account management team has clients that purchased for the right reasons."*

—DERIK SUTTON, VICE PRESIDENT, MARKETING, AUTOBOOKS

"For many people, sales is either some version of order taking or persuading people to purchase something they may or may not need. Bob reclaims the heart of all great sales: empathetic understanding of what people need and giving them just the right solution to a problem. Using a JTBD approach, Bob helps us see the how and why of people's purchasing process, and that will fundamentally change how you engage your customers, how you train your people, how you market. If you are an entrepreneur, an aspiring business-person, and CEO, you need this knowledge."

—PAUL LEBLANC, PRESIDENT, SOUTHERN NEW HAMPSHIRE UNIVERSITY

"Immediately intuitive but incredibly rich; thinking in Jobs moves you from anecdotes wrapped in business jargon to casual insights in the language of your customers."

—ANDY WEISBECKER, SENIOR DIRECTOR, DIGITAL EXPERIENCE, TARGET CORPORATION

"The world of business creates, builds, and sells products and services based on attributes, averages, and correlations. The problem is people are not average and their demographics don't cause them to buy your product. People buy things based on a struggling moment, their current context, their future desired outcomes and trade-offs

they are willing to make at the moment. Bob Moesta has taken these simple observations and flipped the lens on the world of sales. This book builds on my foundations from The End of Average, and uses cause and effect (not correlations) to build a set of frameworks and tools to change how companies see a customer from just WHO they are to a wider set of data including WHEN they struggle, WHERE they struggle, and WHY, thus changing how sales, marketing, and customer support interact with each other and the customer. This book will not only change the way you structure your organizations and sell but change the way you as an individual buy in the future."

—TODD ROSE, PROFESSOR AT THE HARVARD
GRADUATE SCHOOL OF EDUCATION AND AUTHOR OF
THE BESTSELLING BOOK, *THE END OF AVERAGE*

"Selling is not a dirty word, yet all too often the traditional academy has treated it as such. It is a lifelong pursuit—the last mile that connects humans and brings us all together. And yet we receive far too little education in how to do it well. Bob Moesta has been thinking about how to do sales well for years—by helping customers make progress. This is the first product in a groundbreaking effort to peel back the layers to selling effectively—something we all do every single day of our lives."

—MICHAEL B. HORN, COAUTHOR, *CHOOSING COLLEGE* AND
CO-FOUNDER OF THE CLAYTON CHRISTENSEN INSTITUTE

"Sales have always been such a critical component of any successful startup company but are rarely if ever, taught in academia. There are very few sales professors. Why is that? This book fills a much-needed gap by enabling sales to get back to the core of business education. This is our first chance to start teaching basic principles to prepare entrepreneurs and future business leaders on how to navigate the complexity of sales."

—MIKE BELSITO, CO-FOUNDER OF PRODUCT COLLECTIVE; ADJUNCT PROFESSOR OF DESIGN AND INNOVATION AT CASE WESTERN RESERVE UNIVERSITY

"As an investor and advisor of early-stage ventures, I am always looking for ways to help my companies accelerate sales growth and lower customer acquisition costs. I've been applying Bob and Greg's Jobs to Be Done sales framework for years and it has proven to be the most powerful and broadly applicable I've ever seen. This book has packaged complex topics into a consumable format and is a must-read for anyone in sales."

—ANDREW GLASER, MANAGING PARTNER, LASER VENTURES

"The Jobs to be Done theory will change the way you think about sales. But more importantly, the theory will change the way you think about life. It is a beautiful masterpiece because, at its core, it's simply about helping people make progress. And what could be more noble than that?"

—EFOSA OJOMO, GLOBAL PROSPERITY LEAD, CLAYTON CHRISTENSEN INSTITUTE

"This book proves that just because a company can make something, doesn't mean that they should! I love the notion that Bob shares around creating products based on the struggles that consumers are experiencing and the white space that is created when you understand consumer demand and the hacks that consumers have created to meet it. As a product developer, demand-side sales enable us to design the right product for consumers, trading off frivolous features and benefits. This book is a game-changer for teams that want to create products with consumer value."

—LAUREN LACKEY, PRESIDENT, CENTAURI INNOVATIONS; FORMER VP OF R&D, PRODUCT DEVELOPMENT CONSULTANT

"Jobs to be Done theory, and specifically Bob's method of applying it, has been transformational for me in my professional development. His simple but elegant framework, the Forces of Progress, is one of the most useful tools I've learned in my career—and personal life. These concepts are going to be so useful to the sales profession—a fundamental reset on purpose and practice."

—JAY GERHART, DIRECTOR OF INNOVATION, ATRIUM HEALTH

"At some top business schools, we struggle to effectively teach sales—indeed, there continues to be a raging debate about whether sales can be taught. Leave it to an engineer like Bob to show us how. Whether you are looking to learn sales or teach it, Bob's book should be essential reading."

—ETHAN BERNSTEIN, THE EDWARD W. CONARD ASSOCIATE PROFESSOR OF BUSINESS ADMINISTRATION, HARVARD BUSINESS SCHOOL

DEMAND-SIDE SALES 101

DEMAND-SIDE SALES

STOP SELLING
AND HELP YOUR
CUSTOMERS
MAKE PROGRESS

BOB MOESTA *with Greg Engle*

FOREWORD BY JASON FRIED

LIONCREST
PUBLISHING

DEMAND-SIDE SALES 101

Stop Selling and Help Your Customers Make Progress

ISBN   978-1-5445-0998-3 *Hardcover*

       978-1-5445-0996-9 *Paperback*

       978-1-5445-0997-6 *Ebook*

       978-1-5445-1470-3 *Audiobook*

To my teacher, mentor, advisor, and most of all my friend: Professor Clayton Christensen (1952-2020). Rest in peace, my friend!

CONTENTS

"People rarely buy what the company thinks it's selling."

PETER DRUCKER, FATHER OF MODERN MANAGEMENT

The thread that led us to write this book!

FOREWORD

BY JASON FRIED

I learned sales at fifteen.

I was working at a small shoe store in Deerfield, Illinois, where I grew up. I loved sneakers. I was a sneakerhead before that phrase was coined.

I literally studied shoes. The designs, the designers, the brands, the technologies, the subtle improvements in this year's model over last year's.

I knew it all, but there was one thing I didn't know: nothing I knew mattered. Sure it mattered to me, but my job was to sell shoes. I wasn't selling shoes to sneaker freaks like me; I was selling shoes to everyday customers. Shoes weren't the center of their universe.

And I wasn't alone. The companies that made the shoes didn't have a clue how to sell shoes either.

Companies would send in reps to teach the salespeople all about the new models. They'd rattle off technical advancements. They'd talk about new breakthroughs in ethylene-vinyl acetate (EVA) which made the shoes more comfortable. They'd talk about flex grooves and heel counters and Texon boards. Insoles, outsoles, midsoles.

And I'd be pumped. Now I knew everything I needed to know to sell the hell out of these things.

But when customers came in, and I demonstrated my mastery of the subject, they'd leave without buying anything. I could show off, but I couldn't sell.

It wasn't until my manager encouraged me to shut up, watch, and listen. Give people space, observe what they're interested in, keep an eye on their behavior, and be genuinely curious about what they wanted for themselves, not what I wanted for them. Essentially, stop selling and start listening.

I noticed that when people browsed shoes on a wall, they'd pick a few up and bounce them around in their hand to get a sense of the heft and feel. Shoes go on your feet, but people picked the shoe with their hands. If it didn't feel good in the hand, it never made it to their foot.

I noticed that if someone liked a shoe, they put it on the ground next to their foot. They didn't want to try it on yet, they simply wanted to see what it looked like from above. Companies spend all this time making the side of the shoe look great, but from the wearer's perspective, it's the top of the shoe against their pants (or socks or legs) that seems to have an outsized influence on the buying decision.

I noticed that when people finally got around to trying on a shoe, they'd lightly jump up and down on it, or move side-to-side, simulating some sort of pseudo physical activity. They were trying to see if the shoe "felt right." They didn't care what the cushioning technology was, only that it was comfortable. It wasn't about if it "fit right," it was about if it "rubbed wrong" or "hurt" or felt "too hard."

And hardly anyone picked a shoe for what it was intended for. Runners picked running shoes, sure, but lots of people picked running shoes to wear all day. They have the most cushion, they're generally the most comfortable. And lots of people picked shoes purely based on color. "I like green" was enough to turn someone away from a blue shoe that fit them better.

Turns out, people had different reasons for picking shoes. Different reasons than my reasons, and far different reasons than the brand's reasons. Hardly anyone cared about this foam vs. that foam, or this kind of rubber vs. that kind. They didn't care about the precise weight, or that this brand shaved 0.5 oz off the model this year compared to last. They didn't care what the color was called, only that they liked it (or didn't). The technical qualities weren't important—in fact, they were irrelevant.

I was selling all wrong.

And that's really what this book is about. The revelation that sales isn't about selling what you want to sell, or even what you, as a salesperson, would want to buy. Selling isn't about you. Great sales requires a complete devotion to being curious about other people. Their reasons, not your reasons. And it's surely not about your commission, it's about their progress.

Fast forward twenty-five years.

Today I don't sell shoes, I sell software. Or do I?

It's true that I run a software company that makes project management software called Basecamp. And so, you'd think we sell software. I sure did! But once you meet Bob Moesta and Greg Engle, you realize you probably don't sell what you think you sell. And your customers probably don't think of you the way you think of yourself. And you almost certainly don't know who your competition really is.

Over the years, Bob's become a mentor to me. He's taught us to see with new eyes and hear with new ears. To go deeper. To not just take surface answers as truth. But to dig for the how and the why—the causation. To understand what really moves someone to want to make a move. To understand the events that drive the purchase process, and to listen intently to the language customers use when they describe their struggles. To detect their energy and feel its influence on their decisions.

Everyone's struggling with something, and that's where the opportunity lies to help people make progress. Sure, people have projects, and software can help people manage those projects, but people don't have a "project management problem." That's too broad. Bob taught us to dig until we hit a seam of true understanding. Project management is a label, it's not a struggle.

People struggle to know where a project stands. People struggle to maintain accountability across teams. People struggle to know who's working on what, and when those things will be done. People struggle with presenting a professional appearance with clients. People struggle to keep everything organized in one place so people know where things are. People struggle to communicate clearly so they don't have to repeat themselves. People struggle to cover their ass and document decisions, so they aren't held liable if a client says something wasn't delivered as promised. That's the deep down stuff, the real struggles.

Bob taught us how to think differently about how we talk, market, and listen. And Basecamp is significantly better off for it. We've not only changed how we present Basecamp, but we've changed how we build Basecamp. We approach design and development differently now that we know how to dig. It's amazing how things can change once you see the world through a new lens.

Sales is everything. It's survival. From selling a product, to selling a potential hire on the opportunity to join your company, to selling an idea internally, to selling your partner on this restaurant vs. that one, sales touches everything. If you want to be good at everything else, you better get good at this. Bob and Greg will show you how.

INTRODUCTION

My apprehensive leap into sales and marketing began twenty years ago, when I took a startup from $500,000 to $18 million in a short twenty months. But it started out miserably...

As an engineer—a real geek at heart—I had little notion of what sales encompassed when I stepped into my first sales role. I thought of sales as a series of techniques, tools, and processes—a trade—and I just had to learn it. So, it's with this mindset that I boldly took a lead sales and marketing role at a home products company manufacturing and selling solid surface countertops for kitchens and bathrooms, my second startup. I was excited about our product—a new type of kitchen countertop—and believed that if I understood how my product worked and its position in the marketplace, I would strategically know how to sell it. Tell people about the product, and they'll buy it, right? The idea was that we sold our countertops to small kitchen and bath shops, as well as big box retailers like Lowe's and Home Depot, who in turn, sold direct to the customer. Easier said than done.

Immediately, I struggled! This felt more like art than science: people, emotions, exceptions—no equations, very scary. The hair on the back of my neck went up whenever I encountered someone because I thought of every person I met as a prospective customer, all the time. To me, the consumer world seemed irrational and random—like falling into a blackhole—very different from engineering. Previously, I'd been responsible for solving problems for people, but in sales, I was trying to get something from people—money in exchange for my product. For some reason, sales felt icky. It was an unnatural "push" to get people to buy my product. I knew I hated pushy salespeople, and I didn't want people to hate me. I didn't know if I wanted to do this and wondered if sales had to be this way. I considered myself more of an introvert at the time, and most salespeople seemed to be extroverts. I felt like I was a misfit in the true sense of the word. When I did procure a lead, the rules of engagement were murky, and I was directed to say and do whatever was necessary to close the deal.

I began to make trade-offs, compromising on both sides of the table—with the customer and internally with the company: if they wanted black, well then I'd figure out black. I caused havoc back at the office. The customers were managing me and our process, where I felt I had been reduced to an order taker. My confidence waned. I wrestled with how to sell directly to the resellers and meet their needs, versus providing what the end-user customers wanted. I felt my loyalties pushed and squeezed. I had loyalty to the company and the customer. But how could I satisfy both? I also felt a huge amount of pressure to grow the business. I'm a goal-oriented person, but it got to the point where I was not sure I could do it anymore.

I thought the problem was my sales technique. Since I had no real sales training, I began to consume everything I could: listening to books, going to seminars, and signing up for classes. Right away, I noticed that I could only find basic sales techniques, such as how to make cold calls or how to get past the gatekeeper, how to do a sales pitch and how to negotiate a contract. There were gaps in how to apply the knowledge in practice.

So, I sought out a sales coach. At the time, I was stunned to find that none of the top business schools in the country even had professors in the area of sales. Lawyers were teaching sales negotiating. Sales management was being taught as part of the human resources curriculum because it was seen as motivation and compensation. I'd studied at both Boston College and the Harvard Business School, and neither had professors in sales. Why didn't I have a sales class? Why are there no sales professors? The short answer: "Sales is a trade, not a profession like accounting or law," I was told. You learn on the job; there is no sales theory.

WHY ARE THERE NO SALES PROFESSORS?

As I puzzled over this, my research pointed me to a moment in time—the 1985 sale of Nabisco—as a possible reason. RJR Reynolds, the tobacco company, bought Nabisco for $4.9 billion—more than its cashflow. At the time, the numbers didn't make any sense. It was the first notion of brand equity: the idea that because people knew the Nabisco brand and their Nilla Wafers, they wouldn't have to sell future products as hard. Prior to this, marketing was viewed as an assist to sales, and sales were measured in cash flow. The moment brands became more valuable than cash flow, marketers grew in power.

By the time I went to business school in 1995, there was plenty of marketing and talk of brand equity, but nobody was talking about sales anymore. Salespeople had been reduced to what I call "order takers," not a trade, just a process people followed. There was no real management theory behind sales, just a set of tools, techniques, and processes—a trade. Sales became to marketing what accounting is to finance—one and the same. The kicker: marketing got a line item on the balance sheet known as "brand equity." They could expense all the advertising and still get credit for the cashflow. They also had sophisticated analysis methods that could be taught in business schools.

As of 2020, there are some elite universities that are bringing sales back to higher education in a sophisticated way—a hybrid of psychology and design—but they've been missing for the past thirty years.

FLIPPING THE LENS ON SALES

It was around this time that I met Bob Ericson, one of our sales representatives—formerly a lineman for the San Francisco

49'ers, a massive man standing at six feet ten inches tall and weighing over 300 pounds—and he kept telling me that I was going about this the wrong way.

"You've got to understand where they're coming from," he'd say.

"But I don't! I don't know what it's like to be a buyer at Home Depot. I don't know what it's like to own a kitchen and bath store. I don't know why the customer wants a black countertop."

"Why don't you go live in their stores for a few days?" he asked. "You will learn a ton."

So, I did. I went to Home Depot and volunteered in kitchen designs, quoting kitchens on Saturdays and Sundays, for several months. And it was my ah-ha moment; I quickly realized I had no idea what I was talking about! Sitting in the back of the vast Home Depot weekend after weekend, I suddenly realized it wasn't about my product at all—it was about the customer.

Our countertops filled a void in the marketplace. At the time, in the late 1990s, consumers had three basic options: low-end laminate, followed by Corian and granite at the high-end. Our product filled the gap between the low-end laminate and the high-end options. Traditionally, consumers had to trade off between high-end cabinets paired with cheap countertops or the opposite; most couldn't afford both. Our product gave them the best of both worlds. It was engineered stone, with the look of Corian and between the two extremes in cost.

Customers struggled to choose from the one-by-one inch, countertop sample sizes. It was hard to pull out colors and match them to the large cabinet doors. Yet, our competitors used these same tiny samples. When I simply switched our sample sizes to two-by-two inches, our product stood out. I also realized that the wide spectrum of color options confused the customer—some brands had upwards of fifty. Four shades of beige just confused people. We had originally planned to expand our palette, but I realized fewer, great options would outperform. In this setting, more wasn't better, just more overwhelming. These two simple steps—making bigger sample sizes and fewer colors options—resonated with the buyer. For the first time, I saw the direct impact of solving a struggling moment in the setting of sales. I had flipped the lens on how I saw sales. Sales started to feel more like engineering—solving a problem—and less icky.

On the business to business side, one of the biggest problems stores had with our countertops was quoting. There were several elaborate measurements, and every store did it differently. Immediately, I streamlined the process. It didn't matter if we got the numbers exactly right. It mattered that regardless, we lived by the quote and that it was easy to create. Right away salespeople began selling our products—they were just easier to quote.

I realized it wasn't just about the product and what it did—the buying process mattered too. There were a lot of details wrapped around the process that when managed correctly, could make us more valuable, like the samples and quoting. Yet, none of the books taught me to look at sales this way—through the buyer's eyes. They were all about building a persona of an ideal, imagined customer. And, in my experience, the imagined customer had little in common with reality. The sales techniques taught in books didn't work in practice for me.

The idea of having a cold lead, where I pitched a preplanned presentation of features and benefits to a persona and not a real buyer, frustrated me to no end. A sales funnel based on the probability someone will buy, without understanding what causes them to buy, made no sense to me. In my experience, customers bought on their terms. I didn't convince them to do anything; they convinced themselves. It was their moment of struggle that became the seed that caused customers to switch to my product or service. We are all creatures of habit, and we will keep doing what we have been doing unless we have that struggling moment. So I flipped the lens, stopped trying to push my product, and started to understand what caused people to pull new things into their lives.

Once I started focusing on the customer—their problem, outcomes, and trade-offs—as well as gave the resellers tools to inform the customer better, sales soared. Flipping the lens from pushing product to creating pull for our solution changed my perspective. And, I no longer felt like a used car salesman, compromising left and right. There's a different way to sell, and it starts with helping people make progress.

As of today, I've successfully launched over 3,500 products and services across various industries in both business-to-business and business-to-consumer situations and have created seven start-ups. Along the way, I took this methodology for designing and building new products and architected a theory called "Jobs to be Done," (JTBD) with my friend and colleague, Clayton Christensen of the Harvard Business School. *JTBD is the theory that people don't buy products, they hire them to make progress in their life.* Together, we created this theory and it helped me build better products. Then I realized it could be applied to the sales process and understanding how people buy as well.

The goal of this book is to reframe the way **YOU** think of sales—to flip your lens and perspective. Great salespeople don't walk around in a sharkskin suit, selling for the sake of profit. Great salespeople are real people: they ask questions, they listen, they learn, and they help you make progress in your life. Salespeople help customers solve problems and make progress in their life. Instead of pushing their product, they represent their product and how it fits into your life. Sales is about perspective—think concierge, mentor, or a coach, not an order taker. It's about looking through your customer's eyes, seeing what they see, hearing what they hear, and understanding what they mean.

And there's nothing icky about helping people. Period! The world could use a little more help.

MY UNIQUE WORLDVIEW

Perhaps my ability to teach myself to reframe sales and to see the world through this unique lens was a result of the fact that my entire life has been about seeing the world from a different perspective.

Growing up, I was a magnet for adventure and sometimes trouble. I fought "wars" with my makeshift, conduit swords and rode my bike off the garage roof for fun. By seven, I had already experienced three closed head traumas that had an impact on my ability to think and learn. Luckily, I was blessed with an unbelievable mother! She was a Detroit schoolteacher and single mom raising four kids alone. As such, she quickly realized the impact of my injuries. While I was uniquely smart in some ways, there were now things I just couldn't do at all.

In grade school, I memorized entire books after they were read to me—think *Go Dog Go*. This made everyone think I could read when I couldn't. Around third grade, during a parent teacher conference, my mom and my teacher caught on. Busted!

"You really can't read, can you?" my mom questioned. And I finally admitted it.

The diagnosis was that I had a form of dyslexia. I don't see anything linearly. When I see a page or a paragraph, I see the spaces first, then I see the bigger words—but not all together, in pieces. I take these broken letters and string words together. My mom, who was a remedial reading teacher, taught me to read with a big, red teacher's pen. I would open a book, circle the five largest words in a paragraph, and then I'd connect the content to create meaning.

My disability dramatically shaped the person I am today, because it forced me to create new abilities—to see patterns in limited sets of data and use that to innovate. I was the boy in my garage always tinkering around, trying to make something out of nothing. I'd spend hours sorting through discarded junk and scrap—broken TVs, arc welders, pumps, speakers—taking them down to their bits and pieces and transforming other people's trash into my new creations. It was an unconventional childhood, and these were my toys. But in the academic world, it wasn't so simple. The focus was on my weaknesses and a hard push to meet the definition of average. Spelling, for instance, was tremendously hard for me. I remember spending hour after hour, year after year studying. Eventually, as an adult, I just gave up. I realized focusing on my weaknesses to fit into the corporate world was not going to work for me.

My struggles became the seed for me to become an innovator and to develop a whole new set of skills and methods. I found a different pathway. My work ethic became my strength, because

I had to work ten times harder than the average person just to fit in. If something seemed impossible, I never quit—thanks to my mother. I assumed it was my own failure and kept at it. As a student, Ds were normal; I saw it as a sign that I just needed to iterate more, learn, and explore. I funneled these character strengths into my passion for science, math, and creating things. And my creations were fueled by my unique perspective. When I see a flower, I don't see a flower—I see the seed, to the stem, to the flower. I see the flower opening, and closing, and the context wrapped around it, similar to how I see words. Ultimately, I see things in time and space, which gives me a unique advantage.

When I was eventually dropped into the world of sales and marketing at the countertop company, and found sales challenging, I decided to dive in and work the problem ten times harder. As I puzzled over it, I realized the focus was always on the product's features and benefits. The customer was a set of demographics: age, zip code, income, etc., but that's not what *causes* people to buy. Their age and location say nothing about what's going on in their lives. To me, these demographics seemed like static pieces hanging in space, disconnected. I needed to connect the dots, go back to the "garage" and piece them together.

When I started interviewing customers in Home Depot, on the surface, there seemed to be endless situational reasons, infinite even. I realized if I could group customers into a few categories of causation, I could figure out how to come in at just the right time and place in the buying process and help them, as opposed to pushing my product. So, I dug a little deeper. When I asked someone *why*, I stopped taking their surface answer. When asked the right questions, the causes for buyers shrunk dramatically—there were just five reasons my kitchen-countertop customers bought. My discovery netted me great success for the home products company; but at the time, I didn't realize I had stumbled across something much larger than a way to sell countertops.

WHAT CAUSES PEOPLE TO BUY?

My mentor, Dr. Genichi Taguchi, always said, "Don't confuse correlation with causation," and it's a concept that's stuck with me throughout my career.

For instance, ice cream and sunglasses sales are correlated. Does this mean you should open an ice cream shop and sell sunglasses? They are correlated, but one's about heat and the other is about the sun. Ice cream sales and drownings are also correlated. Ice cream kills people? Obviously, not! Correlation is not causation. Correlation is surface knowledge and causation is truth. The world of marketing is dominated by correlation. Once you understand true causation, you have night-vision goggles. The JTBD theory when applied to sales is a method for understanding what causes people to buy, as opposed to what correlates with your product or service.

The JTBD theory works across industries, products, and services at scale. There really are **NOT** infinite reasons a person will purchase a product or service, nor is there just one reason.

There are sets of causes—probably only four or five, pathways, patterns, or jobs. Most seasoned salespeople know the causation of their product or services; that's what makes them great. This is my hack, so I didn't have to fail for years before getting better at sales. This was true of my Home Depot customers, and it's been true for the thousands of products and services I've worked on since. I solved the puzzle of sales by looking at it like the intricate parts of a flower, or deconstructed words in paragraphs. My disability helped create my super abilities—pattern recognition. I instinctively understood the causality of the buyer to their products and developed a framework for how people buy. It's not a prescriptive way to sell or a rigid process that tries to convince people with gimmicks and techniques. People convince themselves; we convince them of nothing. JTBD is a theory of how people buy, and demand-side sales is a method for building a sales program around JTBD.

But I've not done it alone! Now I'm in my seventh startup—Rewired—with my partner and co-founder Greg Engle. Greg and I have worked on developing and launching products in this framework for the past seventeen years. At Rewired, we design, develop, and provide management consulting services that help companies develop and launch new products. Greg and I work side-by-side with our clients to help them understand buyer behaviors and build the right go-to-market strategy. While I've taught this theory in the classroom—I'm an adjunct lecturer at the Northwestern Kellogg School of Management and a guest lecturer at the Harvard Business School—Greg and I finally decided it was time to slow down and share our knowledge on a larger scale. The stories and ideas presented in this book are a combination of our collective experiences.

ARE YOU STRUGGLING WITH SALES OR PROGRESS?

The struggling moment is the seed for all innovation! This book is primarily for people who find themselves stuck. They are struggling with the idea of sales. If you are knocking it out of the park, then you already have your value code—this book is not for you. But if you are like I was at thirty-four, and sales feels icky, uncomfortable, and artificially social, this book is for you.

This book is for salespeople selling directly to customers, but struggling in doing so. It's for the salesperson trying to sell to other businesses but failing to land accounts. And beyond traditional businesses, it can be applied to healthcare professionals who need to convince patients about a particular care regimen, or non-profits, such as church pastors, on how to increase attendance and donations.

The title "salesperson" has gotten a bad reputation. People tend to remember bad experiences, such as buying a car and being pushed by an aggressive salesperson focused on their profit, not the customer's struggle. One bad apple has ruined the bunch! But great salespeople don't sell; they help. They listen, understand what you want to achieve, and help you achieve it. A better title would be "concierge."

This book teaches my time-tested theory of sales. It provides you a language to actively talk about sales in a more meaningful way, one based on reality instead of focusing on the "church of finance." It's a fundamentally different way to see the world and once you flip the lens, you won't be able to unsee it. It will not only change the way you sell, but it will change the way you buy. You will become more purposeful and understand *why*. You will see it's about a struggling moment. And you'll learn it's not about you, it's about their progress. It will teach you to listen more intently, be more curious, and truly understand what your customers are saying. Through our collective experiences, Greg and I will lay out an operating framework, so you can apply the theory to your own product or services.

There's this underlying theme: nobody wants to be sold to, but everybody wants to buy. But the reality is that great salespeople help customers make progress in their lives, on their terms. They are helpful, empowering, curious, and creative. They create win-win situations! Salespeople are the lifeblood of any organization. Let us teach you how to stop selling and start helping people make progress in their lives.

Warning: by consuming this book you will not be able to unsee the frameworks and theory of JTBD. The implication is that you will never see a simple purchase the same way again. You will challenge yourself and the people around you to think about these decisions on a much deeper level: Why are you buying this? What progress are you trying to make? What are your new desired outcomes? It's our hope that it will make you a better consumer of products and services in your life by allowing you to make more meaningful decisions.

CHAPTER ONE

TWO PERSPECTIVES ON THE WORLD: SUPPLY AND DEMAND

"Experience by itself teaches nothing...Without theory, experience has no meaning. Without theory, one has no questions to ask. Hence, without theory, there is no learning."

WILLIAM EDWARDS DEMING, STATISTICIAN
AND BUSINESS CONSULTANT

Through the years of developing new products and selling them, I have come to believe there are two dominant perspectives that drive the language and process for a business: the supply-side and demand-side. The notion of supply and demand drive how we see the world, what is important, and the metrics of success. Yet, they are two very different perspectives. As you will see, we need them both, but traditional sales are mostly focused on supply-side thinking.

Supply—Side vs. Demand—Side Innovation

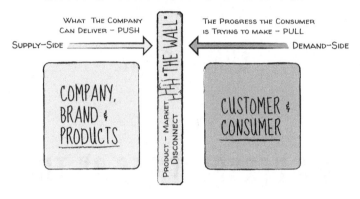

Let's contrast supply and demand with something we can all relate to—purchasing a new mattress. Traditionally, buying a mattress sucks, right? There's foam, spring, pillowtop, and hybrids. There are also different sizes, cooling features, and adjustability. Commissions-based salespeople approach you in an empty store—it's just you, them, and hundreds of beds—and they blatantly push their products using confusing jargon. What are they even saying? So, you stare at hundreds of different models, one costs $1,500 and another $4,000...

"Lay down and pick one," they say.

"I have no idea how to pick one," you think.

It's intimidating! There's almost no way to judge; you're not a mattress expert. How many people want to buy a new mattress but are intimidated by this process?

In 2014, entrepreneur Philip Krim, CEO of Casper, set out to build a different type of mattress-buying experience. He wanted to make purchasing a mattress simple. Instead of variety, Krim decided to only build a few, high quality, foam mattresses. Then the truly novel part, he sucked the air out of his mattresses and shipped them directly to customer's doors. No big box-stores, no aggressive salespeople and jargon, just a few clicks and voila, a bed-in-a-box sitting on your doorstep. And if you don't like it, you have one hundred days to return it. And no, you do not have to get that bed back into the box; they'll come take it away. At the time, industry experts paid little attention to Krim.

Five years later, Casper now has 3.2 percent of the US market share for mattresses—ranking seventh. They've sold to over one million customers with sales topping $400 million and are at a valuation of $1 billion. Meanwhile, industry leaders are barely increasing their market share, and some are even losing it. So, how did this startup come into a well-established industry with lots of competition and become an industry disruptor? It's called demand-side selling, and it's the basis for the JTBD theory of sales. Regardless of whether Casper is ultimately successful, their approach is noteworthy.

SYNCHING SELLING TO THE WAY PEOPLE BUY

Buying is very different than selling. The best sales process mimics the progress that people are trying to make in their lives. Selling is clearly a supply-side perspective, while buying sits on the demand-side.

Instead of thinking about their product's features and bene-fits and asking, "What's the demand for mattresses?" Casper entered the scene and sold sleep. They asked, "How many people struggle to sleep at night?" Their ads feature soft, fuzzy bunnies and kittens crawling across their mattresses, tugging at the sheets. "We asked these creatures of comfort what it's like to sleep on a Casper," the narrator says. "Some things just don't need words." The ad closes with the animals angelically sleeping. Not once do you hear about the features and benefits of a Casper.

What's so special about their approach? It's a worldview of selling from the customer's vantage point, which we call demand-side selling. Casper understood why people buy mattresses and recognized the anxieties that got in the way. And as a result, they designed a better, more simplified way to purchase a mattress. They made buying easy. They gave a few great options, eliminating confusion. They sold mattresses the way people want to buy—risk free and from the comfort of their home. And, in the process, they upset the well-established mattress industry focused on their big, empty box-stores with hundreds of mattresses and confusing jargon.

Traditional sales are not in sync with the way people buy. We need to flip the focus of sales from supply-side selling to demand-side selling. Let's contrast the two.

ONE SIZE DOES NOT FIT ALL

"The tyranny of the average means that we allow ourselves to be stereotyped, striving to fit someone else's idea of who we should be. When we stop comparing ourselves to a non-existent 'average,' the gates just open."

TODD ROSE, AUTHOR, *THE END OF AVERAGE*

Because the supply-side is so worried about efficiency and effectiveness, it's become all about building one model that works for many people. But one size does not fit all! Aiming for average hurts customer satisfaction, because when you strive for average you end up pleasing no one.

For example, buying is very different than selling, just like teaching is very different than learning. Yet in both professions there's a tendency toward a one-size-fits-all approach.

In education there's this notion of a pedagogy—the art and science of teaching. Teachers are taught the best way to teach. Yet in every classroom there are all sorts of different learning styles, just as salespeople are taught the best way to sell based off demographics. Yet buyers are not all motivated to buy for the same reasons.

One size does not fit all in either scenario. There's not one way to sell or one way to teach. But there are also not endless ways to teach and sell. There might be three best ways to do each. It's the "Pareto Principle," also known as the 80/20 rule; 80 percent of the consequences come from 20 percent of the causes.

Supply-side: The focus is on the product or service and its features and benefits. How will I sell it? Who needs my product? You define demand through the product. In this scenario, the consumer is usually nebulous—an imagined, personified version of the customer—an aggregated set of demographic and psychographic information. You aggregate and triangulate the consumer around the product through *correlative* data. When operating under this model you canvas the world for people who need your product, adding features and benefits along the way, to reach the widest audience. With supply-side thinking the focus is on the profit—the product must make money inside a specific cost structure. Everything you talk about goes through the lens of the product or service. You *push* your product. The supply-side does not see how the product fits into people's lives. It's the fishbowl analogy: you cannot see the whole picture swimming on the inside, only what surrounds you.

"Just because I am 55, live in this zip code and have that income, it does not cause me to buy the New York Times today."

CLAYTON CHRISTENSEN, INNOVATION EXPERT
AND HARVARD BUSINESS PROFESSOR

Supply–Side vs. Demand–Side Innovation

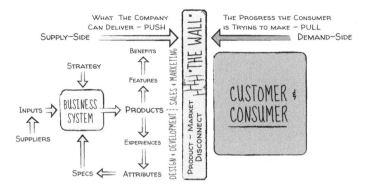

Demand-side: The focus is on understanding the buyer and the user. How do people buy and how do they make progress? What's *causing* them to make a purchase? You design your go-to-market strategy around the buyer's worldview, not the product. You are looking at the world through a real buyer's eyes. It's understanding value from the customer-side of the world, as opposed to the product-side of the world. Demand-side selling is understanding what progress people want to make, and what they are willing to pay to make that progress. Our product or services are merely part of their solution. You create *pull* for your product because you are focused on helping the customer. Demand-side selling starts with the struggling moment. It's the theory that people buy when they have a struggling moment and think, "Maybe, I can do better."

Supply–Side vs. Demand–Side Innovation

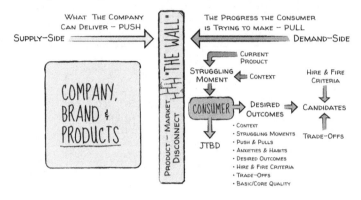

Traditional economics thinks supply and demand are connected. But we would say that demand is independent of supply. Demand is about a fundamental struggle. Supply and demand are two completely different perspectives in sales.

Most people don't think about your product or service if it doesn't address a problem they have. When you're getting a restful eight hours of sleep every night, you don't even notice the mattress store when you walk past. But if you find yourself choosing the recliner every night over tossing and turning in your bed, then you begin to look at—and see—other options. When something's not working the *struggling moment* occurs. It forces people to stop and ask themselves a question. It's those questions that spur demand. When you study how people buy, you realize if there's no struggle, there's no demand—without demand people don't buy. Once you see sales through this lens, you can help people buy and make progress in their lives.

"Questions are places in your mind where answers fit. If you haven't asked the question, the answer has nowhere to go. It hits your mind and bounces right off. You have to ask the question—you have to want to know—in order to open up the space for the answer to fit."

CLAYTON CHRISTENSEN, INNOVATION EXPERT
AND HARVARD BUSINESS PROFESSOR

Supply-side and demand-side together make a business work. The key to synching these two world views starts with understanding demand without the product or your solution—just the context and desired outcomes, tradeoffs, and hiring requirements. Understanding the consumer at a very deep and empathetic level adds more value to the sales approach than focusing only on your product and its features and benefits. Because once you understand the customer, you see patterns and can now define the go-to-market approach based on causation, not correlation. What causes your customers to buy, not how many people are available because of their demographics?

SUPPLY-SIDE VS. DEMAND-SIDE INNOVATION

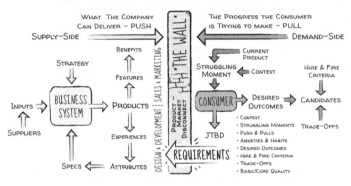

UNDERSTANDING YOUR CUSTOMER'S WORLDVIEW

So, what does it take to become a billion-dollar industry disruptor like Casper? It starts with listening to your customer and truly understanding their needs. It's not only what they say, but how they say it, what they don't say, and what they eliminate. Greg and I walk through this process every day. We identify struggling moments and then reframe products or services from the customer's vantage point—demand-side selling. In the process, we learn to help customers and consumers make progress in their lives.

DEFINING A PERSON'S STATUS RELATIVE TO THE SUPPLY-SIDE...

Lead: A person with a correlative relationship to your product or service, who has the potential to want it.

Prospect: A person who has a struggling moment, wants to make progress, but hasn't figured it out yet.

Customer: The person who buys your product or service and has a set of expectations as a result.

Consumer: The person who uses your product or service to make progress.

Note: Sometimes the customer and consumer are not the same person. Think of a company that buys software for their employees to use or a parent who buys a toy for their child. In these instances, the customer and the consumer are not the same person. The product must be designed for the people who buy it and for people to use it.

A perfect demonstration of the transformative effect of a demand-side sales approach is the story of Paul LeBlanc, president of Southern New Hampshire University (SNHU), and how he transformed SNHU into a billion-dollar public (not-for-profit) educational institution through demand-side sales.

The story begins in 2010 when LeBlanc attended an event Professor Clayton Christensen was hosting at the Harvard Business School. Clay and I were speaking about the JTBD theory—now almost twenty years old—by demonstrating a few case studies. At the time, the SNHU's marketing and sales message was simple: "We've got online classes; you can take them at any time." Like most, SNHU sold their school to prospective students by focusing on their product and services—classes offered and a university degree. The process treated the online school as an extension of the physical school, yet LeBlanc's takeaway from our talk was that the students attending each might be different and potentially had a different set of causes on why they came and sought an online education at SNHU.

LeBlanc took a huge step back and together we interviewed some existing online students to understand their motives— see what they saw, hear what they heard, and feel what they felt. Why did they choose online school? Why now? What barriers stood in their way? Demand-side sales always starts with understanding the people who already bought and made progress with your product or service and then seeing the patterns to help others who have not made the progress yet.

We found that the typical online student was over thirty, working a day job, and often supporting a family in some way. Meanwhile, the students attending the physical school usually began at eighteen, fresh out of high school, and lived a more carefree existence. If you think about where you're at emotionally at eighteen, it's very different—it's a sense of freedom. Our interviews provided a detailed look at the life of the typical online student. We found they had life experiences and responsibilities which were challenging to fit into studying, yet they were willing to sacrifice nights, weekends, and sleep to learn. Why? Because they wanted to secure a better life for their families; a step-up—a career—not just a job. They were motivated internally because they knew they had to change their station in life. They were making the choice from an emotional place and not focused on the university's features and benefits. As we listened and understood, we thought, "There are five hundred online students, but how many more people want to go back to school, but can't figure out how to do it? It's a big market!"

CHOOSING COLLEGE

My friend, educator Michael Horn, and I then took the work we did with LeBlanc and expanded it beyond SNHU and wrote a book called *Choosing College*. The book strips away the noise and helps you understand why you're going to school: What's driving you? What are you trying to accomplish? Once you know *why*, the book helps you make better choices.

The research found in *Choosing College* illustrates that picking a school is complicated. By constructing more than two hundred mini-documentaries of how students chose between different postsecondary educational experiences, Horn and I explored the motivations for *how* and *why* people make their decisions, delving into the subject on a much deeper, causal level. By the end, you'll know why you're going and what you're really chasing.

To learn more, visit Amazon: *Choosing College: How to Make Better Learning Decisions Throughout Your Life*.

JOBS TO BE DONE FOR STUDENTS HIRING HIGHER EDUCATION

01 Help Me Get into My Best School

02 Help Me Do What's Expected of Me

03 Help Me Get Away

04 Help Me Step It Up

05 Help Me Extend Myself

LeBlanc launched an ad campaign targeting these potential students in this moment of their life. It took an emotional approach, resonating with the message of, "It's possible." The ad started with a single parent, working a hard, hourly job, struggling to meet the financial needs of their family—wanting more. It showed the sacrifices, late nights and weekends studying, contrasted against the feeling of pride. It's the emotional story of the satisfaction they'd feel in this accomplishment. You see the character's struggles and feel their success when they finally start their new job—a new chapter in their life. The ad was not about what they'd study, or how the university ranked, but about the journey the online student would go through. It almost contradicted traditional advertising, which says, "We have the highest graduation rate, the best stats." It said, "We can help you get to where you want to go."

SNHU was one of the first schools to strategically target this online market. Their competition was nothing. When prospective students saw the ad they thought, "I'm either going to do this or nothing; do I go or not go?" The ad ran for a month and SNHU received thousands of applications—at least ten times their normal volume at that time!

But once they got these applications, there was a second problem. They couldn't process the high quantities fast enough. It took months. They didn't have enough staff to quickly verify them. The prospective students would see the ad, have a gut response and sign up on a Friday and by Monday morning they were asking, "When will I know if I got in?" Months later when the university would finally get back to these people, they had changed their minds. The energy behind the emotional response to the ad was gone. We realized they needed to figure out how to process the applications faster—in days not months. So, we put a small admissions team together to design a new application process that fit the unique needs of the online students, while dramatically increasing the response time.

As part of the new, faster admissions process, LeBlanc and our team recognized that the application itself was a stumbling block. The average, prospective student couldn't figure out how to even apply. The traditional path, SAT/ACT scores, securing transcripts, and writing an essay served as a barrier. Most had no idea where to find their transcripts; they were not coming directly from high school with a system to help funnel them through admissions. So, rather than having students submit test results and transcripts, the online process started with an interview, where admissions verbally gathered the pertinent details—past academics and financials. Then admissions would gather the documents themselves. This solved a struggling moment for prospective students. Remember, these were working people; they didn't have much free time, and they didn't even know where to find the documentation. The schools already knew exactly what to do.

As SNHU built the process out, more and more people were attracted to the program. They realized there were way more people who wanted to learn online and by the way, it was cheaper to teach this way. The university was able to lower costs, which allowed them to provide these admissions services. Within seven days of applying, they were able to tell prospective students their options—academically and financially—and enroll them. It kept the momentum going!

But another problem emerged. The retention rate started to drop. They found that about halfway through the school year life would get in the way and students would start to drop out. They started with the right intentions but couldn't sustain it. So, we spent quite a bit of time and energy trying to figure out how to help them get through the rough patches. This time, LeBlanc turned to the academic advisors, whose typical job includes helping students pick classes, and flipped them into life coaches. They would monitor the students as they went through the process reminding them exactly why they were doing this. They became the angel sitting on their shoulder, seeing when they hit a rough spot, and providing a bit of confidence or a helping hand: tutor, work group, or somebody to help them through it. It cut the dropout rate by almost ninety percent.

In 2010, there were five hundred online students. Flipping the focus from supply-side thinking to demand-side thinking created exponential growth. In a short ten years, LeBlanc's online enrollment ballooned to 130,000 students. He went from a $100-million university to over a billion-dollar university!

SNHU Results

ENROLLMENT	2010	2012	2014	2016	2018
TRADITIONAL STUDENTS	2,500	2,750	2,912	3,015	3,913
ONLINE STUDENTS	>500	17,000	35,000	60,000	130,000+
REVENUE	$109M	$166M	$352M	$574M	$1.2B

	MAY 2016 GRADUATION	MAY 2018 GRADUATION
	+9,221	+19,761

THE EVOLUTION OF SALES

Before 1943, there was no management theory of business. Zero. At Ford, everybody reported to Henry Ford—three thousand direct reports; a CEO gave orders, and everyone followed. During this time period, a business philosopher named Peter Drucker entered the scene and upended corporate America with his new ideas of decentralization. He sat down with Alfred Sloan of General Motors (GM), and remodeled GM by focusing on power structures, political environments, information flow, decision-making, and managerial autonomy. By shifting power, he was able to replicate their systems leading to immense growth. Now GM had a typical, modern-day business structure: human resources, accounting, legal, engineering, manufacturing, operations, facilities, marketing, and sales.

Back in Drucker's day, sales differed greatly from the role today; it was simple. The traveling salesperson went from town to town selling goods. The demand for everything was great. Salespeople predominantly served as order takers—fulfilling demand—because options were limited. If you wanted to sell a car, you displayed it. Buyers could not easily educate themselves on the options available and relied on salespeople to help them.

While the power structurers architected by Drucker remain largely in place today, the role of a salesperson has changed dramatically. Today, information is readily available, competition is fierce, and consumers are well-educated. As a result, salespeople are dealing with an entirely different buyer. They don't walk into a dealership waiting to be sold to. They live in the age of information. But a new problem has emerged. Consumers are overwhelmed and inundated with information, more confused than ever. As a result, buyers today struggle to find solutions to their problems. Sales must evolve!

THE STRUGGLING MOMENT

The struggling moment is the seed for all new sales. By understanding this, LeBlanc didn't have to convince anybody to buy anything. The prospective students convinced themselves—demand-side selling. If you talk the way the customer thinks, selling becomes easy. You create *pull* for your product. How do you do this? By listening, understanding, and figuring out the contexts and outcomes that drive people to buy. SNHU and Casper both became industry disruptors and made it big by listening to their customers and selling the progress their customer wanted to make. Twenty years ago, selling countertops, I did the same.

If you take the time to listen and truly understand, you will quickly realize it's not about your product's features and benefits; it's about the customer's struggling moment and the outcome they seek. How do the problem and the solution play together? There's a yin and yang; the push and pull. Companies get sucked into thinking about the features the customer wants, as opposed to the outcomes they're seeking. It's the basic premise of cause and effect. Understanding the context by which people value your product will make it easier for you to understand how to sell your product. Only your customer can determine your value!

MAKING IT REAL

- On the demand-side think of two or three examples where you tried to buy and the seller spoke from the supply-side, in sharp contrast to your demand-side buying. For example, you bought a new camera and they sold you shutter speed and zoom, while you just wanted to take a picture of your kid playing soccer.
- On the supply-side think about your product or services. What supply-side language are you using? What demand-side language is your customer using?

Now that you understand the difference between supply-side selling and demand-side selling, let's build the foundational elements of a demand-side sales approach so you can begin applying it to your own product or service.

CHAPTER TWO

THE FRAMEWORKS FOR DEMAND-SIDE SELLING

"People don't want to buy a quarter-inch drill. They want a quarter-inch hole!"

THEODORE LEVITT, PROFESSOR,
HARVARD BUSINESS SCHOOL

Imagine yourself in the Home Depot or Lowe's and you need a drill. You go to the drill aisle and there are drills of every color, with different torques, battery life, and accessories. What's happening here? The guys in Milwaukee are looking at their competitor at DeWalt saying, "They just increased their battery life by 3 percent, we need to keep up." This feature creep, or incremental innovation, does very little to help move the product. It is more about "keeping up with the Joneses" than creating something the consumer can value. This is a supply-side push of technology. Now when you walk down the drill aisle you have side-by-side products that are hardly discernible. How do we break out of this mold? By understanding the progress people are trying to make when they buy a drill. People buy a drill to make a hole, right? We keep trying to sell people the drill, when the reality is, we should be helping them figure out how to drill the hole.

In marketing and sales, there's the push to add a bunch of features and benefits that don't bring any value. We get so myopic on the little things that we don't realize the bigger purpose of what people are trying to do. We should be asking *why*, and not just once but several times. We need to get to the root of the progress people are trying to make.

"I need a drill, because I want a hole."

"I need a hole, because I want a plug."

"I need a plug, because I want a lamp."

"Why do you want a lamp?"

"Because it's hard to see, and I want to read better."

Now, we are beginning to understand the customer. They don't need a drill at all; they need a Kindle. Let's invent the Kindle. Demand-side sales is about taking a step back to see how your products and services fit into people's lives and the outcomes they are seeking.

THE FIVE WHYS

When I was eighteen years old, I had an internship at Ford and went to Japan where I learned the age-old problem-solving technique called the "Five Whys," developed in the 1970s by Sakichi Toyoda, founder of Toyota. It is used to quickly get to the root of a problem. It's the idea that when a problem occurs you should ask *why* five times to find the source of the problem. This method is still used at Toyota today.

Part of the "Five Whys" is to take a step back and not talk about what the customer wants from the solution perspective. For example, people might say I want the car door to be easy to open and close. Now, if you focus on the door, you have a limited set of solutions. As opposed to looking at it more broadly and thinking about making it easier to get in and out of the car generally. Now you are not just looking at the door but the placement of the seatbelt, etc., because you stop assuming you know the solution. It's about seeing the bigger picture.

We use this methodology when interviewing our customers to get to the root of the problem they are trying to solve. Companies are selling drills instead of holes because they do not ask *why* enough times. They sit in boardrooms thinking of their product's features and benefits and fail to see how it fits into their customer's lives because they simply fail to ask *why*. You cannot design the way your customer makes progress; you need to understand their definition of progress and design your process around it. People don't buy products; they hire them to make progress in their lives.

A JTBD IS...

...THE PROGRESS THAT A PERSON IS TRYING TO MAKE IN A PARTICULAR STRUGGLING CIRCUMSTANCE.

Let's define JTBD. It starts when people are in a struggling circumstance, and they want to make progress. Take the above graphic for instance. The person needs to cross the river: their circumstance—so they can get to the other side: the progress they want to make. There are one thousand different ways we could help them cross the river: teach them to swim, build a boat or a bridge, fly a plane, and so on. But building their solution starts with understanding their situation and *why* they are thinking about making progress in the first place, as well as what their vision of progress looks like.

Sometimes people start with a struggling circumstance but have no idea what the other side looks like. Say your parents complain about their house being too big, they hate shoveling snow, and the taxes are too high. It's not a real struggling moment until they figure out what they want to do about it. What progress do they want to make? Typically, this is where people will complain but not do anything about it. The best thing to do here is to take them to a condo and show them what progress looks like, not hire a snowplow. Eliminating the struggle is not progress, them overcoming the struggle is progress. Both pieces are critical; the key to understanding causation is found in the circumstance and the outcome. Value is relative to your circumstance and determined by where you start compared to where you end. Circumstance is a big part of understanding causation. Their circumstance is a reference point for their progress, without understanding their starting place you cannot design their progress.

Great sales begins with understanding the JTBD by your customer and the progress they are trying to make: What is the situation they are in? What's the outcome they seek? What are the tradeoffs they are willing to make? We do this by interviewing people who've purchased your product or services and understanding *why*. And *why* is relative to what's going on in their life that caused them to say, "Today's the day..." But it's not an imagined customer or persona as we explained in chapter one, it's real buyers. And the *why* you are looking for has nothing to do with your features and benefits. It's about the customer and the progress they are trying to make in their life. To build a meaningful understanding of *why* people buy, we must create language, a story, and a model of their struggling moment.

We are going to introduce three key frameworks for how people buy:

1. The three sources of energy or motivation (functional, emotional, and social)
2. The four forces of progress (push, pull, anxiety, and habit forces)
3. The JTBD timeline (sequence of events and actions to make progress)

THE THREE SOURCES OF ENERGY—TYPES OF MOTIVATIONS FOR PROGRESS

There are three different categories of motivation: functional, emotional, and social. Let's discuss how each of the three play out in the buying process. Think of it as the energy or fuel to make the buying process happen.

1. **Functional Motivation.** How cumbersome is the purchasing process for the buyer—time, effort, and speed? I think of mechanical things here: speed, effort, steps, etc. Remember the online students at SNHU? They were working full-time jobs and trying to go to school at night. They had little time to take the ACT/SAT and fill out a laborious application with an essay. They had no idea how to obtain a transcript. Wrapped up in the decision to go back to school were these functional barriers that stood in the

way. We needed to reduce this functional barrier. It was a force pushing them away from our services.

2. **Emotional Motivation.** What positive or negative internal thoughts are driving my purchase—fears, frustrations, and desires? The online students were not focused on the university's ranking. Remember it was the vision of a better life that drove them to suffer through the lost nights and weekends. They wanted to provide a better life for their family. So, our advertisement painted that picture. It showed the struggling moment that people face working a dead-end job. It showed the hard work and the better life ahead. The advertisement focused on the emotional satisfaction they would feel providing for their families.

3. **Social Motivation.** How do other people perceive, respect, trust, or acknowledge me? The online students wanted that feeling of pride the diploma would create. They envisioned just how proud their family and friends would be. And, as a result, how proud they would feel about themselves. Our advertisement painted that picture as well.

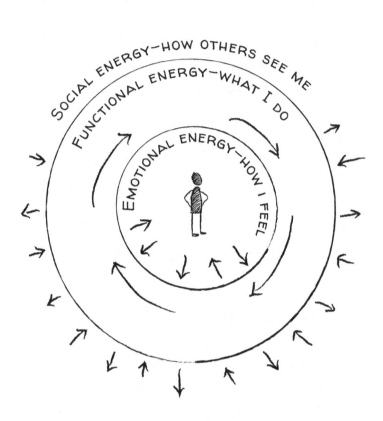

Overall, the goal in demand-side sales is to reduce the negative functional, emotional, and social motivations, which are causing anxiety and serving as a barrier. While at the same time, amplifying the positive motivations to create pull for the product or service.

THE FOUR FORCES OF PROGRESS

One of the methods that we use to unpack causality are the forces of progress. The forces at play determine whether people can move from A to B and make progress. Will it be business as usual or a new path forward? Within the forces are things that *pull* people toward change and frictions that *push* them back to the old. Buying is not random! When we talk about consumers' decisions, we've found there are ultimately four forces driving their progress.

1. **The push of the situation.** If you think about the struggling moment for the person buying a mattress, it's about needing a better night's sleep. They are tossing and turning and it's affecting their productivity during the day—the push.
2. **The magnetism of the new solution.** The moment you realize that something might bring you a better night's sleep and help you make progress, that solution creates magnetism and you start to imagine a better life with a good night's sleep. A friend buys a new mattress and raves to you about it. The pull toward progress.
3. **The anxiety of the new solution.** Despite the problem and the pull the new solution creates, there's anxiety. Will the new mattress deliver on its promise? Can I even figure out which mattress is the best? What happens if I get the new mattress and I hate it? These anxieties hold people back from making the progress that they need.
4. **The habit of the present.** You are used to the old mattress, even though it sucks. You've learned to live with it. There's an energy in that incumbent solution that keeps you from making progress and stops you from switching.

Any time we talk to consumers about a purchase or switch

that they made, we're constantly probing for the forces of progress. The push of the situation and the magnetism of the new solution need to be stronger than their anxieties and habits before they will buy. What levers can we pull to get them to switch to our product? As product developers we think about the first two forces—the push and the magnetism of our product—a lot. We imagine the next big feature we're going to bolt onto our product, which everyone will love. But we ignore everything else—the anxieties and the pull of habit. Our experience has taught us that the money is made on the anxiety side of the equation. If you can figure out what's holding people back, you can shortcut the sales process and really increase profits. We've seen it time and time again. It's how Casper entered the well-established mattress industry and upset the status quo.

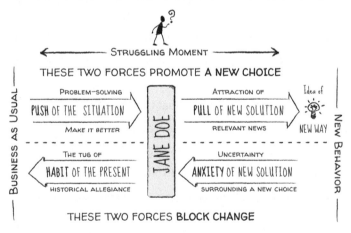

CAUSATION — JTBD FORCES OF PROGRESS

←——————— STRUGGLING MOMENT ———————→

THESE TWO FORCES PROMOTE **A NEW CHOICE**

BUSINESS AS USUAL

PROBLEM-SOLVING
PUSH OF THE SITUATION
MAKE IT BETTER

ATTRACTION OF
PULL OF NEW SOLUTION
RELEVANT NEWS

Idea of
NEW WAY

JANE DOE

THE TUG OF
HABIT OF THE PRESENT
HISTORICAL ALLEGIANCE

UNCERTAINTY
ANXIETY OF NEW SOLUTION
SURROUNDING A NEW CHOICE

NEW BEHAVIOR

THESE TWO FORCES **BLOCK CHANGE**

Notice the above graphic. On the left-hand side we are thinking of the past, which is the current situation and the lack of solution—the problem. On the right-hand side we are thinking about the future and what you want to happen—the outcomes. A JTBD is both the problem and the outcomes. The solution falls in the middle on the graphic. Now if you look at it horizontally, the top is more about the motivating factor moving you forward, while the bottom is about the hindering forces holding you back. By seeing the world in this way, progress now becomes a system, an equation $(F_1 + F_2) > (F_3 + F_4)$. People only make progress when force one and force two are bigger than force three and force four. What we are taught in business school is to add more features, but the forces work as a system and sometimes more features is not better because it causes more anxiety. The ultimate thing is to see the way the customer buys as a system that plays out over a timeline.

THE TIMELINE FOR PROGRESS

The forces and the motivations drive the buyer's decisions, but not in a vacuum. Like any good crime, there's a timeline. Yet, traditional sales teaches you that the buyer is just a set of demographics: zip code, income, age, etc. We've already learned how oversimplified this thought process is. But even if you dig deep, and understand the forces and motivations at play, it's not the full picture. The buyer must also be in the right time and place in their life. Nothing is random! Through the years we've uncovered the six stages a buyer must walk through before making a purchase:

1. First Thought—creating the space in the brain
2. Passive Looking—learning
3. Active Looking—seeing the possibilities
4. Deciding—making the trade-offs and establishing value
5. Onboarding—the act of doing the JTBD, meeting expectations and delivering satisfaction and value
6. Ongoing Use—building the habit

JTBD TIMELINE – THE PROCESS OF MAKING PROGRESS

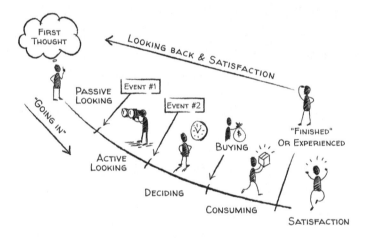

There are events that move people along the timeline. When conducting interviews, we imagine the events in their life like huge dominoes falling. We need to understand the buyer at a very granular level. What happened that made them say, "Today's the day I am going to…"? We need to understand *causality.* What are the events which pushed and pulled them to move forward or backward? It is an important concept. The customer has a certain set of systems for how they buy, and our process needs to feed their world to help them make progress. So when interviewing, we continue until we can imagine the dominoes in their life tipping over, moving them along the timeline.

FIRST THOUGHT

When you finally have that first thought: "I'm not sleeping well," or "This is a dead-end job." Whether you say it out loud, or you have it in your head, it's the critical first step for you to buy. Before this first step, there's not a place in your mind to file the information about mattresses or online universities. The thought process around buying is complicated.

Once you have the first thought, you've opened up the space

in your mind for the information. Without this first thought there is no demand. But once you have it, you notice things you didn't notice before, which causes you to transition to passive looking.

Four ways to create a first thought

1. Ask a good question…and not give an answer
2. Tell a story
3. Give a new metric
4. State the obvious

PASSIVE LOOKING

You notice the mattress store when you pass it now. You drive past a local university and wonder if they have online classes. You have passed these places every day without a second thought, but now, like Clay Christensen said, the questions in your head create spaces to file this information. The first thought is how you create the space. Passive looking is how you start to fill the space. People can passively look for years if there's no event pushing them to the next step on the timeline. Maybe you have a big meeting, sleep horribly, and underperform the next day. Now you might say to yourself, "Today I need a new mattress." This event is like a domino falling in your life that moves you along the timeline to active looking.

Recently, a friend bought a mattress at Costco on a Saturday while shopping with his two kids. On the surface he seemed to do it on a whim. "It was an impulse purchase." But we know nothing is random, so I questioned him a little further.

"So how long haven't you been able to sleep?"

"For two years," he said.

His first thought happened two years ago. But the positive forces toward change were not bigger than the anxieties and the habit of the current situation. Two years later, something happened that pushed him into active looking. The Costco mattress was in the right time and place in his life. Like my friend, consumers often can't explain *why* they bought something, but with the right questions you can connect the dots for them and understand how to help them make progress.

Passive looking is the act of figuring it out as you go through life. You have a hole, a nagging feeling, you are struggling, but you don't know enough to move forward. It feels random. You must decide if the struggle is big enough to warrant moving forward while determining if a solution even exists to solve your problem. Passive looking is about learning. Learning the problem, learning the language, taking the temperature of people around you, and socializing it. It's usually done alone and you're not purposeful about it but more opportunistic— there's no effort, no time or money set aside to figure it out yet. The moment people start planning, they are in active looking.

ACTIVE LOOKING

Active looking is when people plan, or spend time and even money figuring out what's next—the solution to their struggling moment. In order to make progress and move forward people need options, but not too many, as a reference point. These options allow them to start to build an ideal solution in their mind.

Now buyers also need a second event, a domino, before they can move to the next step on the timeline. We call this event a "time wall." It can be artificial, or not, but it's the fabricated notion that they must make their purchase by a certain date. If there's no time wall, people might look forever. But the moment the time wall is established, people buy. For example, "We hired a builder for the kitchen remodel, and he needs the countertops next month." It doesn't matter if they're buying software, countertops, or mattresses, there must be an imposed timeline. Companies often run sales for this reason, but you must be careful not to overdo it, which causes you to lose the urgency.

Active looking is where people start to invest time, effort, and thought to see the possibilities. They notice discrete, independent features and attributes and start connecting the dots to frame future tradeoffs. Active looking is about divergent thinking and eliminating things. However, people are still abstract in their thinking—they're still learning. They start to invest time, money, and effort to figure it out and often bring other people into their thought process during this stage.

DECIDING

Here's where people make their tradeoffs and ultimately decide what they want. When buying, there's no ideal solution, and every customer makes tradeoffs. Part of the journey in sales is understanding the tradeoffs your customers are willing to make. When I sold kitchen countertops, I could send customers to look at the low-end laminate and the high-end granite. These were clear reference points for people to compare our product to. Without these comparisons, people struggle to buy. People need to reject something before they can buy something else.

Realizing what people are willing to give up in order to make progress is the most powerful part. People will say they want the top-of-the-line mattress, or the best kitchen cabinets and countertops, but when it comes down to it, nobody gets everything they want. People make tradeoffs. You need to know what tradeoffs your buyer is willing to make.

Deciding is where people connect the dots and realize they can't have it all. It is also where they make explicit tradeoffs between things they value. The expectations for satisfaction are cemented while they decide, and value is defined. The customer's understanding of quality, performance, and satisfaction start here, and everything in the future is measured based on the final expectations locked while they are deciding.

WHAT IS A TRADEOFF?

The traditional notion of a tradeoff is a set of "compromises." But in the setting of sales that's not how we would define a tradeoff. We think of tradeoffs as, "I can have it this way; I can have it that way; or I can not have it at all." It's choosing the best way to make progress, as opposed to just a compromise.

For instance, people either want thick crust pizza or thin crust pizza. If you averaged those results, you'd get medium-thick crust pizza—nobody wants that. Using the average does not work! By forcing people to choose thick or thin, you make it easier for them to decide. They like one or the other; it's easy for them to eliminate one from these two very different options.

A tradeoff in the setting of sales is more about helping people make better decisions than compromises. When tradeoffs are framed well it becomes easy to make decisions. When they are not framed well people can't decide and they do nothing. Tradeoffs are the key to helping people buy.

ONBOARDING

Onboarding is where the rubber hits the road. It's where the consumer determines if you've met the expectations set when they decided to lock-in and buy your product or service. Whatever expectations were set are now poured in concrete. In onboarding, the consumer is having their first use of the product or service and measuring that against their expectations to see if they bought what they think they bought. Here's where it's important that the metrics set in deciding are the right metrics; otherwise the consumer will be dissatisfied and have buyer's remorse.

Onboarding can be thought of as the "big hire," or buying the product or service, whereas ongoing use are the "little hires" associated with the consumer incorporating the product or service into their everyday life.

ONGOING USE

There's a difference between buying and onboarding a product or service and using a product or service everyday—ongoing use. In fact, most think of buying and onboarding as the beginning, but we always think of it as the end of part one in a journey to make progress. In ongoing use, the consumer decides if a product or service is doing the job through a series of repeated little hires each time they use the product or service. How well did we satisfy expectations? The satisfaction is determined by the expectations we set in part one. If you did not set expectations well, the consumer will have new struggling moments, which over time can lead to a new big hire. Ongoing use is where the jobs get done and the progress is achieved.

As a simple example, let's use Windex. Onboarding, the big hire, is buying the bottle of Windex and the first use of the product. Ongoing use, little hires, is squirting the bottle of Windex as part of your routine cleaning. How well does it work over time?

DESIGNING PRODUCTS FOR BIG AND LITTLE HIRES

At the beginning of my career as an engineer, I would design the best "little hire" moments, but nobody would buy my product. I found myself always building stuff that nobody bought because I was designing them with only the little hires in mind. Then once I started designing for the "big hires" I never had enough money left over to design for the little hires.

What do I mean? Think of Salesforce. The big hire is bought by the VP of sales, marketing, and IT. They are the ones deciding to increase the information system. But the salespeople are the little hires, the people who use the product every day. If Salesforce gets the big hire right but fails to be user friendly, slowing people down, the product will fail because ultimately sales will go down.

When you design a product, you need to build it to be bought and used. You must focus on both the big and little hire. Salespeople screw up when they over promise and under deliver. We need to match the expectations when buying with what we deliver, not over promise and underdeliver.

Pulling together the forces, motivations, and timeline allows you to see the buyer as a whole person. They are no longer a set of demographics; they are real people. By understanding the buyer in this way, you can begin to design a demand-side sales process.

SEEING THE WHOLE: WHY DO PEOPLE BUY?

The key frameworks outlined in this chapter connect the customer's implicit systems for buying to the supply-side's systems of sales, marketing, and customer success. When pulled together, these elements will enable you to sell in a way that helps the customer make progress in their life.

We will teach you how to think like the customer: to see, unpack, and connect the demand-side of buying to the supply-side of selling. Once you see what they see and hear what they hear, you will be able to connect the customer's phases for buying with each of the departments in your organization. By organizing your sales, marketing, and customer support system to the customer's system for making progress, the departments within your organization will be able to work together as one seamless system.

Progress is the goal of this book, and organizational alignment the side effect! When you connect the dots between your organization and the customer's system of buying, helping the customer make progress will naturally follow. Additionally, approaching the customer from this vantage point will accelerate your customer's ability to make that progress. But it all starts with understanding the customer's JTBD, the triggers, and the micro-progress at each phase in the customer's timeline. The following graphic is a snapshot of how your departments will align to the customer's systems for buying.

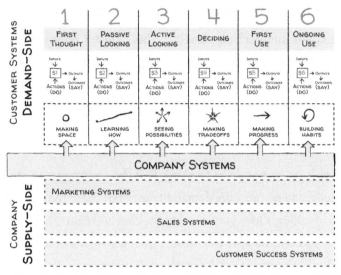

DEMAND-SIDE SALES IS ABOUT HELPING YOUR CUSTOMER MAKE PROGRESS

MAKING IT REAL

- On the demand-side, use the forces, motivations, and timeline to map out a recent purchase you made. What were the forces at play? What positive or negative motivations contributed to your decision? How did you move along the timeline?

- On the supply-side, use the timeline to describe how somebody bought your product or service.

Now that we have the bones of the framework for demand-side sales, let's look at how these components play out in a real-life example.

CHAPTER THREE

SOLVING THE CUSTOMER'S STRUGGLE

In 2004, I decided to apply my skillset in sales, marketing, and engineering to a local business where I could make an investment. A small, regional home builder based out of Detroit was a natural fit. When I joined the company, they built close to a hundred houses annually. I told them I would partner as an investor over time, but I wanted to spend a year learning about the business first. So, I became the vice president of sales and marketing.

Our top competitor was a large, national home builder who sold significantly more volume than us. With my engineering background, I walked in with the ability to influence how the homes were designed, reducing costs, as well as sales and marketing—the hard part.

Right away, I was shocked! The sales process was based off the assumption that people who bought new, never looked at used. "Nobody who wants to buy new is looking at a used house ever?" I questioned. I knew this could not be accurate. Additionally, salespeople pitched the homes using the same, preplanned presentation for every prospect regardless of their circumstance. A customer would walk in the door, be briefly greeted, then given a presentation which consisted of a litany of features and benefits. Most people walked away and stopped listening after about three minutes.

"Well, let me tell you about Elk Trail. Elk Trail is a community of two hundred and thirty houses that's 37 percent finished, and we've got fifteen houses that are up for sale, blah, blah, blah."

They'd run through this presentation without asking any questions: Why are you moving? What's going on in your life? And this was the standard approach across all new real estate sales; our large, national competitors had the same approach. It was in this setting where I met my longtime partner Greg, who had also recently joined me at this regional homebuilder.

"What the heck is going on here?" we both questioned. Greg came with an extensive background in sales in both food and electronics retailing. He was fresh off a big growth effort that had ended in a company running out of cash and quickly into bankruptcy. Their loss and our gain. We hit it off from the beginning.

RETHINKING THE SALES PROCESS

We decided to start by talking to homeowners who had bought houses from us over the last six months. Greg and I would take a couple of pizzas, some soda, and a flip chart to their home and interview them. We would draw a line down the center of the chart and begin.

"This is today, and here is where you had the first thought of buying. Now, tell us the story. How in the world did you get to the point where you bought this house?" we'd ask.

At first, people would say they couldn't remember, but there are techniques we can use to jog their memory. We wanted specific details: What knowledge did they have along the way? When did they have this knowledge? How did the knowledge impact their decision? But we didn't ask those questions directly. We'd often say something casual to set the tone: "Imagine, we want to shoot a documentary about how you decided to buy this house." Then we'd start from their move-in day, walking the conversation backwards through the timeline. As we went along, we started to understand the thought process homeowners went through.

We were curious, how did the preplanned presentation impact their decision? It turns out, it did not influence their purchase at all. The preplanned presentation, which droned on with a litany of features and benefits—not a deciding factor. Only a third of our preplanned presentation nailed what they wanted.

Another third confused them; they had no idea what we were talking about. And a third would play into their anxieties, pushing them away. "Do I really need all of that?" they'd wonder. So, while the presentation hit on everything imaginable with the intent to reach the broadest audience, overall it actually damaged our chances of selling a house.

UNDERSTANDING THE PUSHES AND PULLS

So, what forces were at play? What was pushing them towards buying? What anxieties were pulling them away from the purchase? How did their allegiance to the past, their old house, play a role? What finally caused them to say: "Today's the day I am going to buy a house?" Simply, we pulled our house out of the solution set; our house did not cause them to buy. So, what did? To find out, we tried to discuss their purchase without talking about our house at all.

"Why did you move?"

"What was going on in your life?"

"What were you hoping to achieve by moving here?"

Each interview took about an hour. They'd talk about their struggling moment. We'd have them draw a picture of the timeline with no words. After ten interviews, we asked ourselves: "What do these stories have in common?" And we'd start to see a pattern. Three of the stories boiled down to a growing family that needed more space—babies, generations moving in together. They wanted help finding a home that would allow them to live together more harmoniously. Another five of the stories were about the opposite—downsizing. They'd tell us about getting older and wanting to travel. The kids had moved out, and they didn't need the space anymore: "I don't want to host the holidays," they'd say. They wanted help figuring out how to downsize.

Those interview patterns showed very consistent forces at play—pushes, pulls, and anxieties. What were they worried about? What were they not worried about? For this example, we will focus on downsizers, a main target audience for this home builder.

The Four Forces

The push of the situation. What's going on in their life that triggered the desire to move? Nobody really wants to pack up their entire house and move. We usually asked, "Why in the world did you need to move now?" The answers varied, but it was not an infinite number of reasons. We would get a laundry list: the house is too big, the kids have moved out, the yard's too much work, the laundry room's in the basement, high taxes, etc.

The magnetism of the new solution. Our brand-new condos

were ideal for these buyers: first floor, two bedrooms, two-and-a-half-bath, first floor laundry. They'd see it, and there's a pull toward it. "What do you like about our condo?" we'd ask. Not surprisingly, they spoke of the newness, updated kitchen, and laundry placement. Often, we'd hear that they wanted to travel more and liked the lack of seclusion—their belongings would be safer.

Anxiety of the new solution. But as they're thinking about everything they love, and the reasons it's perfect, they are also simultaneously thinking of a set of questions and anxieties; panic would kick in:

"How are we going to move?"

"How are we going to sell the house?"

"Where's the grocery store?"

"How are we going to get rid of all the stuff in the basement?" After all, they were downsizers who needed to pack up a 3,000 square foot home and consolidate it into a 1,600 square foot condo.

The habit of the present. There were always a lot of things they loved about their current situation. They had friends and a community. They'd raised their kids there; it's packed full of memories. The habit encourages them to stay put.

Their fears and force of habit would overwhelm their overall appreciation of the condo. So, despite the positives, they'd start to pull away. They needed something to push them to act. There's a push—the magnetism of the new condo—but there's more anxiety than anything else. We could build the best condo in the world, but if the push and the pull are not greater than the anxiety and the habit, they're not going to move. In business school we are taught to add more features and benefits, which would create more magnetism, pushing people to buy our product. It's not true! We've got to reduce their anxiety.

CAUSATION – JTBD FORCES OF PROGRESS

← STRUGGLING MOMENT →

THESE TWO FORCES PROMOTE **A NEW CHOICE**

— BUSINESS AS USUAL —

PROBLEM–SOLVING
PUSH OF THE SITUATION
MAKE IT BETTER

JANE DOE

ATTRACTION OF
PULL OF NEW SOLUTION
RELEVANT NEWS

Idea of
NEW WAY

THE TUG OF
HABIT OF THE PRESENT
HISTORICAL ALLEGIANCE

UNCERTAINTY
ANXIETY OF NEW SOLUTION
SURROUNDING A NEW CHOICE

— NEW BEHAVIOR —

THESE TWO FORCES **BLOCK CHANGE**

The Three Motivations

So, how do we go about doing this? It starts with grouping their positive and negative motivations into three categories—functional, emotional, and social—and stepping in to solve their anxieties within each category.

Functional motivation: Our interviews had established that many of our buyers were downsizing. They had a 3,000 square-foot home and were moving into a 1,600 square-foot condo. They had a lifetime of belongings that they needed to sort through. What stayed and what went? It was a daunting task. Many talked about the challenge of sorting through and packing up their entire life. Wrapped into their home purchase was a plethora of fears and anxieties. They'd get stuck and consider not buying.

Our solution: We raised the price of our condos, built a storage facility across the street, and hired movers to pack their belongings, label their boxes, and move them. We included this service as part of our package. Additionally, we built a clubhouse with a sorting room inside our storage facility. Now when their kids visited, they could all walk across the street, and sort through their lifetime of belongings together at a casual, leisurely pace.

This decision alone increased sales by 22 percent! We solved a functional problem by making it easier to move. Conversely, our competition down the street offered five thousand dollars off and free granite. Did they even want granite? Most buyers could read through this gimmick and understood they just jacked-up their prices.

Emotional motivation: We learned through our interviews that most of the downsizers began thinking about moving during the holidays. As they prepared the Thanksgiving feast for twenty, and set up the decorations for Christmas or Hanukkah, they'd decide they were ready to pass the torch to their children.

"I'm done hosting the holidays," they'd say to themselves. "This is too much work!"

They'd tell us that they only wanted a kitchen bar, where they could have three or four chairs and a small kitchen table. They're downsizing after all; it made perfect sense. What they really wanted was a large second bedroom with a suite for visitors. Yet, when we dug deeper, a consistent theme arose across multiple interviews. What happens to the dining room table?

"Well, my niece Sarah might take the dining room table, then we could move," we heard in one interview. At first, we thought nothing of it. But then it happened again. "My cousin Mac took the dining room table and then we moved." We heard it once, twice, by the end we heard it ten times.

"What's going on with the dining room table?" Greg and I wondered.

Despite everything they said about not hosting the holidays, they were torn. We realized that the dining room table turned out to be the emotional bank account of their lives. They could not just put it in the basement, or into storage; it wasn't going to Goodwill or any old stranger. If they did not know what was going to happen to the dining room table, they were not going to move. So, as much as they told us they wanted a second bedroom with a large suite, it's not what really mattered. Emotionally, they could not move without sorting out the dining room table.

Our solution: We reduced the size of the second bedroom dramatically, gave it a shared bath, and made a small room for the dining room table. We realized that if they did not have a place for the dining room table, they were not going to move. The table represented every birthday, holiday, and special event from their past. It was all tied up emotionally in that table. The moment we added a small room for the table—not functional for hosting anything—sales jumped 27 percent.

We did the opposite of what they told us to do, because of the emotional bank account the dining room table represented.

Social motivations: Our condos appealed to a fifty-five-plus audience who didn't want the chaos of a typical subdivision. Many saw their neighborhoods changing over to young families and now felt out of place. They were socially motivated to live near other people in a similar circumstance. Similarly, when younger families move it's often about wanting their kids in a better school district, near a certain church, etc.

UNDERSTANDING TIME AND PLACE

So, how did we take the knowledge from our interviews and market to people at scale? Sometimes your strategy changes in unexpected ways…

The Timeline

At the home builder, when we interviewed people about their first thought of moving, they often talked about setting up for the holidays.

"I told my husband, we should think about moving next year," said one buyer. "We're doing too much. The kids moved out. We should pass the torch to our children and take it easier on the holidays."

But the holidays came and went. They no longer were having the conversation actively, but because of that first thought, they were now noticing things that they otherwise might not pay attention to—passive looking. "The house down the street went up for sale," they would tell us. "Once we saw that we just up and got a real estate agent."

Remember, nothing is random. So, we wanted to know what the heck happened that made them reach out to a real estate agent? There's no doubt that an event in their lives pushed them from passive looking to active looking. Hiring a real estate agent is active looking. What was it? This is where we would stop and say, "Hold on a second, tell us a little bit more about the agent."

"Oh, we've known her for years. Her name is Sally. She's been a good friend of the family, blah, blah, blah."

"So, when did you sign up?" we'd ask.

"I don't know, February maybe."

"Was it the middle of February, end of February?" we'd question.

"It was the middle of February."

"Near Valentine's Day?"

"No, it was after Valentine's Day."

"All right," we'd say. "Was it during the week or on the weekend?"

"Oh, it was during the week."

"Now, this seems a little strange, but pretend we are shooting a documentary. Sally comes over, right? Did you call Sally? Did Sally call you?"

"Oh, we called Sally."

A favorite technique we use to jog people's memories is to get into the minutia of their life to trigger bigger memories.

"What were you wearing when you signed the documents, and where were you?" we questioned.

"Now I remember! It was a Thursday," and the flood gates opened. "We had just come from a funeral. Our friend Jim passed away. We realized his poor wife would have to move their entire house alone. If we don't move now, one of us is going to have to move without the other, and neither of us wants that to happen. On our way to the funeral parlor, we decided to call Sally."

We heard this story once, twice, ten times. So, we decided to run a test. We moved our advertising from the real estate section to the obituaries. And seemingly overnight, we got a 37 percent increase in traffic and because ad space is cheaper in the obituaries, a 70 percent reduction in costs. The leads were unbelievable. The close rate on those leads was unbelievable because they were already in active looking.

CONTRASTING SUPPLY VERSUS DEMAND

When Greg and I first came into our roles at the regional home builder based in Detroit, salespeople viewed everyone who walked through the door as a prospect. They had a preplanned presentation that talked about our features and benefits at a very high level. It's sales from a product perspective—supply-side sales. As a rule, preplanned presentations tend to get bigger and bigger over time and less and less and less relevant. But once we understood the buyer's timeline and developed questions and answers specific to their position on the timeline, we only needed two minutes instead of twenty:

1. "How long have you been looking?"
2. "Is your house up for sale?"
3. "How's your life going to be better by moving?"

Once we saw the world through the buyer's eyes, we were dramatically more efficient. We could employ just one salesperson per homesite, because we didn't have to talk for twenty minutes about every feature and benefit. Once we knew where they were on the timeline, we could figure out what we had to do to help move them along the timeline. The goal was not to get buyers to jump from the first phase to the fifth. It's not possible! Knowing the customer's stage on the timeline allowed us to talk to them and help them move forward at their pace.

If we pushed too hard at the beginning, we would have turned them off and even scared them away by feeding into their anxieties. Instead, we met them where they were on the timeline. If their house was not up for sale yet, we'd tell them to go online, fill out a survey, and we'd help them get it listed. If they were unsure how much they could afford, we'd look at their debt and give them the answers. Let's build a solution together and help you frame out your options.

How many people want to move but can't figure out the details? If we could help solve their roadblocks and move them through the phases of buying, we were much more likely to sell. We didn't create more things, we took care of their anxieties, which increased the pushes. We recognized that we were not just builders, we were movers! The more we could help people move, the better off we were.

When Greg and I began at the regional home builder, there were seven homesites and one hundred houses sold annually. After switching to a demand-side sales approach, we catapulted the business to fourteen homesites and three hundred homes sold annually. We created pull for our homes by understanding the customers' struggles and meeting them at the right place and time. We figured out how our homes fit into their lives. Greg and I viewed ourselves as a moving company, helping people get from one home to the next, not just a builder. Together, we have now applied this approach to hundreds of companies for both sales and strategy, including innovation and start-up communities.

MAKING IT REAL

- On the demand-side, take a minute and look for struggling moments in your life. What did you buy recently? How did it relate to a struggling moment? Connect the dots between your struggling moment and the purchase.

- On the supply-side, think of your products' or services' features. What are the struggling moments that make these features valuable?

Now that you've seen demand-side sales in action, let's walk through the process step by step with three case studies, starting with the customer interview.

CHAPTER FOUR

SEEING THE WORLD THROUGH THE CUSTOMER'S EYES

The devil is in the details! Wrapped up in the details you will find the social and emotional energy that *caused* someone to buy. Without the little things, the sale never happens. To help people make progress, you must understand *how* other people who bought your product or service before made progress. This starts with interviewing existing customers.

It's natural human behavior to hold back when being questioned; to give the simplest answers to stop the interview. As a result, our interviewing techniques are based more on criminal and intelligence interrogation methods than market research methods and social sciences. You must unpack things from the details, to actions, as well as to when (time) and to space (where). It's the details that enable us to understand what *caused* a person to make progress and buy our product or solution. But the interrogation should feel like a casual conversation, like talking to a friend. Easier said than done.

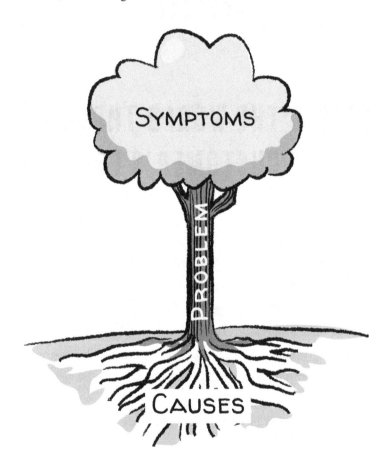

FINDING THE SET OF CAUSES THAT MAKE PROGRESS

Interviewing for *causes* is part art (learned through experience) and part science. It's based more on criminal and intelligence interrogation than traditional interviewing and market research techniques. Short of water boarding, people will lie to you and to themselves. "Buyers are liars!" has always been a saying in the sales world. The reality is that buyers rarely intentionally lie; but, for example, "to get healthy" is not a cause, that's more a wish or a desire. Compare that with causes: "I don't want to die" or "I want to fit into that suit for the wedding next month." The key to interviewing for causes is following a set of principles and tips that act as guardrails for best practices. Also, I recommend reading and re-reading Chris Voss' book *Never Split the Difference*. It's a collection of tools and techniques that take interviewing to the next level—amazing book. And, as such, we can't simply give you a few tips and walk away. First, we'll set the stage with our best interrogation techniques for ensuring interview success. Followed by a demonstration of our interviewing process with three real examples:

- a C-Level executive firing a bank and hiring a replacement
- a person choosing a virtual doctor over urgent care
- someone purchasing a new computer

We will make it look easy, but it's much harder than it appears. The key is to practice.

THE FIVE KEY PRINCIPLES

It's important to keep these five principles in mind as we move forward with the technique. Think of them as the guardrails that safely keep you on the right path.

1. **Humility: You're not smart enough to instinctively know why people really buy.** Assume nothing! You need to be an investigator to understand the *causal* events that led someone to make a purchase. There are too many causes and too many different sequences, which makes it hard to see patterns. You can't sit in a conference room and figure this out.

2. **Causality: Everything is caused; nothing is random.** The notion of randomness was created to help us be "okay" with no explanation. But it's overused and has the side effect of enabling us to waste time and wait. Home builders will sit in a trailer in the middle of a development waiting for people to randomly stop by. That is insanity! People don't randomly stop by—they stop by with a purpose, but because we don't know when, we don't ask *why*.

3. **Tradeoffs: Everyone makes tradeoffs to make progress.** I'm willing to give up this, so I can get that. No one can have everything. What tradeoffs is your customer willing to make? I have a friend who bought a brand-new Audi RS7—beautiful car. It was silver, and he wanted matte grey. Why did he settle for silver? Because he would have needed to wait another month for the car to get matte grey. He was willing to make a tradeoff to have the car immediately.

Sales is about managing and packaging the tradeoffs the consumer is willing to make.

4. **Disconnected: Most people don't know why they do what they do.** They will tell you a purchase was random, an impulse purchase, or they'll give a simple answer. You need to dig and not accept their surface response. Most people live their lives in the moment and don't connect the dots. "I bought a mattress on an impulse." "So how long haven't you been able to sleep?" "Two years."

5. **Lies: Everybody lies.** You must be careful not to fall for the lies people tell themselves. If someone says, "I bought this product because it's important to be healthy." You should ask them to tell you three other things they've done recently to be healthy. They don't lie with malice or intent. They build a story that fits their world. We call it the cake layer of causality. Lies are a very complicated thing. This is about getting past the lying, past the cake layer.

THE TOP TEN JTBD INTERVIEW TIPS

Next, we have our top ten tips for interviewing…

The setup

Set a casual, conversational tone from the beginning. Ask for first names of people, places, and dates. Almost like you want to shoot a documentary.

Do this: "I'm doing some early research to understand the language people use when talking about buying our product. There's no right or wrong answer. I don't have a long list of questions. This is about helping us understand the words you use, and how you fit our product into your life."	**Don't do that:** "I'm doing research. Tell me why you bought this."

It's important they don't feel like there's a right or wrong answer. When set up correctly, the conversation becomes more casual. We truly do not bring a list of questions, because it's not about our product; it's about the buyer's progress. We follow the interview where it takes us and fill in the timeline as we go along. Also, at the start ask the names of key players, like their husband or kids. Then use them later in the interview when you ask a follow-up question. Suddenly, you're at a different level of familiarity.

Details, details, details

Yes, you're digging for the details, but the details are also how you jog their memory.

Do this: "What was the weather outside?" "Who was with you?" "Did you call them, or did they call you?"	**Don't do that:** "Tell me about the day." General high-level questions do not work.

Asking detailed, specific questions about tangible aspects is a trick to jog an interviewee's memory. Asking innocuous details surrounding their purchase triggers bigger pieces of the puzzle to fall into place. "It was snowing! Oh, now I remember…"

The brain can remember vast details when prompted or surrounded by details.

Context creates meaning

The irrational becomes rational with context. When the answers feel irrational, it's typically because you don't know the whole story. "Hold on I am confused..."

Accept this: "I bought the pizza because our team won the big game, and we all wanted to go out to celebrate."	**Don't accept that:** "I bought the pizza because I like pizza." *Like* is not a cause, it is an excuse for not knowing why.

Most people if asked would say they like steak and pizza, so why did they buy pizza in that moment? Why didn't steak make sense in this context? Context has as much meaning as the product.

Contrast creates value

Providing an interviewee with contrast leads to greater understanding. Have them tell you why they decided against an alternative path. I use a bracketing technique to help provide contrast where neither option is right, and they need to elaborate.

Do this: "Why do it virtually? Why not just get into your car and drive to the doctor?"	**Don't do that:** "Why do it virtually?"

Without giving them contrast they often can't figure out why they did what they did. Ask people to tell you what it's not. Most people can eliminate or tell you what it's not easier than they can tell you what it is.

Unpack vague words

Everything is bound. You are trying to figure out the interviewee's reference point.

Accept this: "It installed fast, in just under two minutes. The last program took five minutes to install."

Don't accept that: "It installed fast."

One person's definition of the word fast may be entirely different than another's. There's no healthy, only healthier than... There's no fast, just faster than...

Energy matters

Listen for the energy. It's not just what they say but how they say it.

Question this: "I bought this new laptop and it's REALLY good." "[Sigh] I bought this laptop and it's good."

Don't question that: "I bought this new laptop, and it's really good."

Do they accentuate words? Does the intonation go up or down? Downward intonation implies there's something wrong. Listen for pauses and sighs. Did you hear a comma, but there is no comma? Did you hear all caps, but there's no caps? As soon as you hear this emotional energy, stop and ask further questions. "Wait, tell me more about that. Why is that important?" When we interview customers, Greg and I focus on how people say things as much as what they say.

Play "dumb"

When you want to question what they're saying, put it as your own stupidity or your naivety. "How much RAM did you get on the new computer?" you might ask. "Well, I don't know," they respond apologetically. In this scenario you need to be able to delve into the topic without making them feel dumb. "I am confused" is one of my favorite sayings…but you have to mean it when you say it.

Do this: "I mean what's RAM anyway? You know what I mean?"   **Don't do that:** "Why don't you know how much RAM you got?"

The moment someone feels stupid they shut down. The moment they think you are judging them they feel insecure. Sometimes interviewees set up a response by saying: "This is really stupid but…" And I will respond: "Oh, I do that all the time."

Set-up bad questions

A lot of times there's a question that is either a little bit too personal or a little too close to the vest. You know that if you don't ask, they will never tell you, so you set it up: "Okay, this is a bad question, don't feel you need to answer it and please make it better."

Do this: "I've got a personal question, and if you don't want to answer it you don't have to, but why were you at the doctor?"	Don't do that: "Why were you at the doctor?"

When you set it up as a bad question, they are always expecting the worst, much worse than the actual question. It disarms them from what might have been a negative or awkward response.

Good cop, bad cop

It always helps to interview in pairs. You don't have to, but when you do, you can play good cop, bad cop.

Do this: Argue with each other to fuel the conversation.	Don't do that: Argue with the interviewee.

Or we play back the story wrong and argue with each other over the details. It's a good way to check what's most important to the interviewee.

Use analogies

Often the interviewee will hit a wall and not have the language to express their thoughts completely. Don't push, but instead use analogies to help build language.

Do this: "How is buying a phone like buying a laptop?"	**Don't do that:** Continue to push in the same way when they are at a loss for words.

Sometimes asking them to compare two things that are not similar at all works well. It forces people to think and use better language.

CASE STUDY EXAMPLES

There's something called the domino effect. It's the idea that a domino can topple over a domino double its size and start a chain reaction. As you read each of the case studies, imagine what dominoes had to fall for people to move forward along the timeline. What forces were at play pushing them toward a new product and pulling them away? To be clear, the following interviews are actual stories, not brainstormed or ideal-user experiences. Seeing the customer from the demand-side will clearly demonstrate the disconnect with supply-side-only thinking. "The irrational becomes rational with context," we always say. People making plans in conference rooms about products are largely rational. Yet, most people do not behave rationally when they buy. Customers make tradeoffs and connect dots emotionally—even when choosing rational services like banking.

The purpose of this section is to demonstrate how we uncover the forces, dominoes, and motivations through a series of questions formed in the moment, not preplanned. Our discussions then act as a guide for the frameworks outlined in chapter two. It's important to not just listen and take surface answers but to unpack the personal meanings behind the language being used. Ultimately, it's about the intent behind the words. Additionally, we listen carefully to not only what people say, but how they say it. You'll see that the same words can be said in completely different ways, which can imply different intents.

As we go through the interviews, we will pause—game off—to discuss what we've learned before continuing forward—game on. These moments of reflection will show what we have learned, and where we are headed next, so that hopefully you will begin to understand the degree of listening, thinking, and adjustment that's required when you conduct your own interviews. We will make it look easy, but it's not. Successfully conducting interviews to understand the causes behind customer's decisions requires practice, like riding a bike. And like riding a bike you can only learn so much before you need to hop on and try it yourself.

CASE STUDY #1: BANKING
What Causes a Bank to Get Fired and a New One Hired?

What makes someone fire a product or service and hire a new one? A struggling moment and a thought: "Maybe I can do better..."

Our first case study is the story of Chad. He owns a biotech company for hospital equipment that he founded in 2009. A short four years later, he fired the initial bank holding his loans and investments. *Why?* We sat down with Chad to uncover his story.

Chad began by giving us the pertinent background information. He acquired the company in 2009 after raising the Series-A Equity—capital from investors—in conjunction with the initial financing. He hired a bank, we'll call them "Bank A," to manage all their holdings. "Bank A" held their loans, totaling about $2 million, as well as their treasury management systems and merchant card services. (Treasury management systems optimize a company's liquidity, while mitigating risk. Merchant card services are for credit card and debit card transactions.)

After four years, in 2013, he fired "Bank A." We asked him to recall back several years to tell us his story, so there are cobwebs around some of the specifics; but when getting someone to recall memory, if it's emotional, it's in there. What forces drove Chad to change banks? What solutions did the new bank offer? What role did Chad's anxieties and forces of habit play in the decision-making process?

Bob *(The setup)*: Chad, we're trying to understand the language people use when they talk about banks. This is early research, so we just want to have a conversation to get your story. Imagine I'm shooting a documentary and I am trying to understand why you switched banks. We're going to ask some weird questions, but we don't have a list. We just want to hear your story.

Bob: At some point, something happened at the old bank that made you say, "Today's the day we're going to switch banks." Tell us about that. At what point did you have the first thought? At what point, in and around the decision in 2012, did you think, "Okay, we have a problem."

Chad: We did a minor acquisition, which we internally financed. But as a result, we needed to restructure our capitalization table. (The capitalization table is a spreadsheet that shows the company's equity ownership).

Bob: So, what happened next?

Chad *(Energy Matters)*: Well, it became very clear that the existing institution did not understand our business **AT ALL**. And more importantly, just didn't have a desire to understand our business!"

Bob *(Unpack vague words)*: What do you mean? How do you know they didn't understand?

Chad: The financial changes were very standard for a life-science business. Yet, we were getting pushed into a cookie-cutter scenario that did not apply to our business. They never tried to understand what we were trying to do, or where we were trying to go. Also, the person we were dealing with was very green, and the third relationship manager we had been assigned in as many years.

Bob *(Unpack vague words)*: What do you mean by third relationship manager?

Chad: The person we started with, who put the facilities in place initially, left and the position had turned over several times.

Bob: Three times?

Chad *(Energy Matters)*: At **LEAST** three times! I had never met this new person face to face. It quickly became clear that this was going to be an arduous process for a minor change. It concerned me, because I knew that in six months we wanted to put new financing in place for capital expenditures for the remainder of that year. (Capital expenditures are funds generally used for a new project.) This headache over a relatively minor change made me very concerned about their ability to handle the bigger financing coming down the pike.

Bob: Are you trying to educate this relationship manager?

Chad: Yes.

Bob (*Details, details, details*): Are you doing this on the phone or email?

Chad: On the phone.

Bob: Are they local?

Chad: Yes, local.

Bob (*Context create meaning*): But he wouldn't come over, or you couldn't go see him?

Chad: Well, I'm not going to go. I mean...

Bob: Just say it. He works for you, right?

Chad: Yes!

Bob: Damn it. He should come to you!

Chad (*Energy Matters*): If they wanted to understand our business, come see our freakin' business.

GAME OFF

THE PHONE IS
DOWN

Can you see the energy here? He uses the word *freakin'*. Why is he so upset? Most people are conflict avoidant, they'd move on. But here's where you need to dig in, it's counterintuitive, but buried with the emotions are the *pushes* of *why* he left the bank. Hear that statement again: "If they wanted to **understand** our business, **come see** our freakin' business." We need to unpack those key words: **understand** and **come see**. Are they the same thing? **Come see** implies he wants a relationship, while **understand** indicates he wants them to know how he makes money. Let's dig in and find out!

GAME ON!

THE PHONE IS
UP!

Bob: Right! He's sitting at his desk listening to you talk, doesn't understand your business, and at some point in time you must be thinking, "I have to explain all of this? Oh my god, really?" Did you invite him over?

Chad *(Energy Matters)*: Oh, **ABSOLUTELY!** We had several phone conversations where we talked about the **EXACT** same information. The conversation would end. Our relationship manager would go back to gather information, so we could talk again in ten days. Ten days later, **NO CALL**. I'd call them and they'd start all over again asking the **EXACT** same questions.

Bob *(Context creates meaning)*: Is there time pressure on your part? Do you need to get this done by a certain date?

Chad: For that job there wasn't a significant amount of time pressure.

Bob: But it's that other thing…

Chad: I knew that the clock was ticking, because I wanted our new capital expenditures facility in place within one hundred days. And if I'm going to switch institutions, well now there is time pressure, because I'll need to repackage the whole deal. There was time pressure in terms of are we staying or going.

Bob: You're not revealing this other plan to him? You must be thinking, "Oh my god! If I add this to the conversation, it'll confuse the crap out of him even more?"

Chad: Well, I'm not trying to be a shitty customer and act like, "Well if you don't get this done, we're out of here."

Bob: You're trying to make it work.

Chad: I'm thinking, "I'm trying to give you more business, and I think this should be a relatively easy thing to get done, but if you're going to put us on the back burner and just not give us an answer, string us along for six months, then that's just not going to work for us."

Bob *(Details, details, details)*: So, imagine I want to shoot the scene of you hanging up the phone and turning to whomever and saying: "Okay, we need to start looking for banks." When did you finally do that? What was the last straw?

Chad: I think it was the second or third phone call where we went over the exact same things again. And I knew we were dealing with somebody who was very green.

Bob *(Context creates meaning)*: Why didn't you elevate it?

Chad: Oh, I tried.

Bob *(Unpack vague words)*: What do you mean you tried?

Chad: I tried.

Bob: What does that mean, you tried?

Chad: I went to the president of the bank and basically was told that I needed to work with this person.

Bob: Wow!

Chad: And at the time, I think we were probably the second or third largest long-term loan they had in their portfolio.

Bob: Is this where you open the flood gates? How do you find the new bank?

Chad: We had just hired a VP of finance. I was in the process of allowing that individual to really own the banking relationship.

Bob: Welcome to the company.

Chad: Yes, exactly.

Bob: Find a new bank.

Clearly, the energy of all three realms—functional, emotional, and social—are at play here. Who said banking is boring and not emotional? We have enough of the back story, but we need to keep digging: How did he find the next bank? Who helped him? Did he hire the new VP based on this banking problem? How did he fire the old bank? What fears are driving his decisions? Keep digging, uncover more! We know the struggling moments, the *pushes*: He wants to grow the business and the bank does not understand him. The bank is rotating through people. They are nickel-and-diming him to save pennies, while he's trying to grow. Let's go to the next side of this.

GAME ON!

THE PHONE IS UP!

Chad: I told him the most important thing was that we have an institution that understands our business.

Bob *(Unpack vague words)*: What does that mean? What are they supposed to know?

Chad: Different businesses have different unique metrics. For instance, what's a receivable, what's not? Is a maintenance contract a receivable? Or is an annual renewal? Do we lend on that? Do we not lend on that? How do we structure that borrowing base? It takes some real in-depth knowledge of a company's contracts; how they renew with their customers, etc.

Bob: Got it.

Chad: Hospitals typically pay slow. I don't think that's a shock to anybody. Our borrowing base is not a standard ninety-day borrowing base. Anything past that, screw you. We have almost zero bad debts, but our borrowing base needs to be 100 to 120 days. If we're at an institution where it's, "This is our standard deal, here's our template. You either fit this or don't." That's not a place for us. And frankly I don't think that's a place for any company.

Bob *(Context creates meaning)*: Who wants that, right? Did you even give them a chance? Did you even tell them that you're shopping?

Chad: I think after the third phone call, I unleashed my VP of finance: "Here's what we need, go look for it. Here, are institutions off the top of my head that you should go talk to; add whoever you want to the list."

Bob: How many banks did he bring you?

Chad: Four.

Bob: Help me understand what these four meetings were like. How do they know what to pitch?

Chad: If I sit down in a meeting of that nature and there's a Power Point presentation already prepared, a deck to sit through, I get up and leave.

Bob *(Context creates meaning)*: Why?

Chad: Because they don't know us. The finalists in that process were the ones who opened up the meeting with, "We're really happy to be here. We want this meeting to be all about us understanding you and your business. And then we're going to go back, put our thinking hats on, and come back with a presentation." As opposed to, "Here's our standard deck that we give to every company, and you're going to fit into one of our three boxes." Ultimately, we ended up with the bank we did because they started from a blank sheet of paper. I also knew that group very well, but I tried to remove myself from the decision.

Bob: But even knowing them very well, they still came in with a blank sheet versus a Power Point?

Chad: Absolutely.

Bob *(Details, details, details)*: And you didn't tell them to come in with a blank sheet?

Chad: No, not at all.

Bob *(Contrast creates value)*: Was there another bank that came in with a blank sheet?

Chad: Yeah, one other.

Bob: The other two of the four, gone right away? So now you're down to two?

Chad: Correct.

Bob: How in the world did you choose? And what was the timing on it?

Chad: Here's the interesting part. The bank we picked was more expensive.

Bob: You bought the more expensive one?

Chad: Absolutely, because the structure of the term facility on the future capital expenditure was much more flexible.

Bob: So, you bought flexibility?

Chad: Absolutely. In terms of features, that's what we cared about.

Bob *(Contrast creates meaning)*: And tell me why the other guys lost.

Chad: My personal relationships certainly played into it.

Bob *(Unpack vague words)*: What does that mean? Tell me more about that.

Chad: Well, I knew that group extremely well.

Bob: What do you mean you knew them?

Chad: I knew the individual who ran that group, I worked for him at Merrill Lynch.

Bob: Okay. Yeah, but working for somebody and knowing somebody...

Chad: I trusted him.

Bob *(Unpack vague words)*: What does that mean? Whoa, trust. It's a big word.

Chad: I trusted that he would tell me things clearly and upfront. Meaning what they can do and what they can't do.

Bob *(Contrast creates value)*: So, wait a second. Give me an example of exactly that. What's something they said, "Yeah, we can do this, but we can't do that." Can you think of a specific causal thing? It was five years ago, so it might be too hard.

Chad: Well, I'll say this, originally when we switched, I personally guaranteed everything.

Bob: Wow!

Chad: And in those conversations, I remember very distinctly asking, "Is there a way that we can structure this, and I can get off as a personal guarantee?" The other bank said, "Well, maybe. Let's look at it. Let's talk about it." Which just means, "No, but we don't want to tell you. We're going to pop that on you two days before closing."

Bob: Or two days after.

Chad: The bank we ended up choosing said, "Nope. Can't do it and if that's a deal breaker, we need to walk away right now."

Bob: Wow! So, I just want to make sure I got this straight. By delivering the bad news in a straight-forward way he earned your trust, because the other guys waffled on it.

Chad: Yeah.

Bob: You want somebody who's going to be direct with you, and trust was earned because he could deliver the bad news.

GAME OFF

THE PHONE IS
DOWN

We got it! We understand the dominoes that had to fall, the pushes and pulls. To clarify, I played the story back to him with minor but significant changes to test my understanding and get some better language. Let's debrief.

CASE STUDY #2: HEALTHCARE

How Do People Choose to Get Help from a Medical Professional?

Greg and I had been working on a project in the on-demand care space. We wanted to understand how customers used those medical services before recommending how to enhance or amend them. So, we recruited a list of patients to interview who'd used these services in the past ninety days. Our first patient was Jen. She had hired virtual care for the first time recently, rather than going to urgent care. We wanted to know *why.* What *caused* Jen to go there? What was she expecting, and did the services meet those expectations?

Bob *(The setup)*: We want to talk to you about some of the services you've had in the last ninety days. If there's anything you don't feel comfortable answering that's fine. We don't have a list of questions. We're trying to understand the language you use as a consumer. Imagine we're shooting a documentary. If we have an actress that's going to play you, what do we tell her to feel like? There are no right or wrong answers.

Bob: Before you start, can you tell us a little bit about you and your family?

Jen: My husband and I have been married for almost twenty years and have a college-aged daughter, Susan. My husband is very technically savvy and is a software engineer.

Bob: What's his first name?

Jen: Kyle. My daughter is also tech savvy, so there's a lot of laughing at me that goes on.

Bob: You're not tech savvy?

Jen: I can make things work, but I have a learning curve.

Bob: You count on them, or you just have them do it for you?

Jen: No, I have them help me troubleshoot when I can't figure it out.

Why in the world do we need to know her husband's name? Because it builds familiarity and ease. If throughout the interview I now refer to him as Kyle, rather than your husband, it's almost as if we are friends. The more you can make people comfortable, the more they are going to reveal the emotional and social aspects behind their decisions. Additionally, she offers up a vulnerability by letting us know that she's not that tech savvy. The more we can lean into this and help her feel comfortable the better.

GAME ON!

THE PHONE IS UP!

Bob: Tell us about the first time you used virtual visit? Do you remember when it was?

Jen: I was very sick; my voice was going. It was a Sunday morning.

Bob *(Details, details, details)*: I almost want you to do a timeline. When? In the fall, the spring?

Jen: Probably February or March timeframe. I had a choice, I could go to urgent care, I could wait and call the doctor on Monday, or try the virtual visit.

Bob *(Details, details, details)*: I want to kind of slow it down a little bit. You had been sick for a while, or you felt it coming on?

Jen: I had been sick for several days by then.

Bob *(Unpack vague words)*: What does that mean, several days?

Jen: Four or five days.

Bob (*Contrast creates value*): Tell me how it started. Did it ramp up, or was it terrible the whole time?

Jen: It started out just like a regular cold. I have asthma, so I started to cough a lot. It got to the point where it was a barky cough and annoying to my coworkers—that's usually what encourages me to go to the doctor.

Bob: Do your coworkers say something to you?

Jen (*Energy matters*): They're like, **"Oh, are you okay?"** You know, after eight hours of sitting next to someone that's barking, **it's annoying!**

Bob (*Context creates meaning*): Just to make sure I got this right, your clue that this is a problem is when somebody says, "Are you okay?"

Jen: Yeah.

Bob: But you still didn't go, why?

Jen: I thought, I'll hang out over the weekend, I'll start to feel better. Then it was Sunday and I realized I would still be barking on Monday. I knew I didn't have time for that.

Bob: It was the notion of going in on Monday still sick? You thought, "Crap"?

Jen: Exactly.

Greg *(Good cop, bad cop)*: You didn't feel bad?

Jen: I felt bad, but that's not usually the thing that will get me to go. It's when it's noticeable to other people.

Greg *(Unpack vague words)*: What does feel bad mean?

Jen: I have less energy. People will notice that I look tired.

Greg: Were you running a fever?

Jen: I might have been. I don't know.

Bob *(Context creates meaning)*: It almost feels like you're too busy to notice. You're coughing but don't really notice. And at some point, people are interrupting you and you think, "Leave me alone, I'm fine"?

Jen: Right.

Bob: Is that an over exaggeration?

Jen: No, not at all.

Bob (*Contrast creates meaning*): Was it more about the fact that you didn't want to bother the people around you at work the next day or that you felt bad?

Jen: Yeah, pretty much. I don't like answering those questions: "Are you okay?" "Have you gone to the doctor yet?"

Bob: You're guilted into going.

Jen: I feel bad but not enough to go by myself.

GAME OFF

THE PHONE IS
DOWN

Wow, so the *push* is not just that she feels bad for several days, it's the fact that people keep asking her about it. She is more worried about how she's perceived than her own health. You start to realize the impact of social pressure; some people need to not only feel bad, but they need other people around them to push them to go to the doctor. I imagine her worrying on Sunday about the response from her coworkers the next day.

She's lost productivity, feels behind, and doesn't want people interrupting her with a barrage of questions about her health on Monday. I understand the social energy here, now let's go back to the timeline.

Bob *(Details, details, details)*: What time do you decide to go?

Jen: Sunday, probably around eight in the morning. I had on my bathrobe. I thought, "Am I going to go to urgent care, or am I going to go do a virtual visit?" I hadn't done one before.

Bob *(Contrast creates value)*: What's the difference between the two?

Jen: In urgent care, you go and wait in the waiting room, then they'll see you without an appointment. Virtual care, if you can figure out how to sign up, can be done from the comfort of your home.

Bob: You don't see anybody physically?

Jen: You see the face of the person on the other end, like Skype.

Bob: Sounds like they're the lesser of two evils.

Jen: Right.

Bob *(Details, details, details)*: How far away is urgent care?

Jen: Probably ten, fifteen minutes.

Bob *(Contrast creates value)*: What was the thought about going there? Was it even a real consideration or was it, "I'm going to do this virtual thing?"

Jen: No, I was going to go. Then I was in my bathrobe and I just didn't feel like getting dressed and going out.

Bob *(Contrast creates value)*: If this had occurred at three o'clock in the afternoon and you were dressed, you probably would have just done urgent care?

Jen: Probably.

Bob: Eight in the morning, still coughing? Are you sitting there with your husband, Kyle?

Jen: Yep.

Bob *(Details, details, details)*: I want to shoot the scene with you and Kyle. Is Kyle telling you to go?

Jen: Yes.

GAME OFF

THE PHONE IS
DOWN

Why am I getting so specific with Jen? Because it's hard for people to remember things when they are not tied to a significantly emotional event. We find that people can remember way more than they think they can if you can get their mind back into the context of the moment. The details help people remember what really happened. So, I am unpacking these details to help her remember. When conducting an interview where the person is hesitant with their answers, deploy this tactic. The more you can get them back in the moment the more the details will flow.

GAME ON!

THE PHONE IS UP!

Bob: If Kyle hadn't told you to go, would you still have gone?

Jen: Yes.

Bob (*Details, details, details*): Again, help me with the scene of you and Kyle. Are you sitting at the table, sitting on the couch, where were you?

Jen: We were in the office.

Bob: What's the conversation?

Jen: "I think I probably need to go take care of this," I said.

Bob (*Details, details, details*): Sorry, I'm going to slow it down more. You walk in, or he walks in, you're already there?

Jen: He's in the room, I come in the room; he's always in there because he works from home. I say, "I feel pretty gross, I think I need to go to the doctor." And he's like, "Yeah, I told you to do that."

Bob: When did he tell you to do that?

Jen: Probably two days before that.

Bob (*Setup bad questions*): This might be a hard question, but is this more about Monday, or is this more about needing to feel better?

Jen: Probably equally both. I don't want to go into another week feeling bad with no plan in sight. I probably wouldn't get around to it through that entire week.

Bob: Right, because you had a full schedule already, you lost your energy Wednesday, Thursday, Friday so you're already behind.

Jen: That's right.

Greg (*Details, details, details*): Is the virtual visit software installed?

Jen: No, I didn't need it before then.

Greg: You're in the middle of being sick.

Jen: Right.

Greg: You're trying to figure this out.

Jen: Right.

Greg *(Good cop, bad cop)*: Come on. Why didn't you just get dressed and go? Sorry, but you're not the tech savvy one, you've declared it. You've got to install this thing.

Jen: I figured if it didn't work, I could still go.

Bob: It's almost like, "I'll try this and if I can't figure it out, I'll just get in the car?"

Jen: Yup.

Bob: You've told us that Kyle is tech savvy. Is Kyle helping?

Jen: No. But I knew if I got stuck Kyle would help.

Bob: You've got a backup then.

Jen: Right.

Bob *(Details, details, details)*: How did you find it?

Jen: I went on the website. I knew about it from work.

Bob: Did you have to search for it? Does it say, click here for virtual care?

Jen: On the website, it has a banner bar up at the top you can click on, it says virtual visit, and it brings up the virtual visit platform.

Bob: Then what happens?

Jen: It says, "Do you need to log in, sign up?" It walks you through the screens.

Bob: Okay. You had not signed up?

Jen: No.

Bob (*Contrast creates value*): Did you know how hard it was to sign up, or how easy it was?

Jen: I had no idea.

Bob: What was your anticipation?

Jen: I thought it was probably going to be a pain, but it wasn't.

Bob (*Details, details, details*): How long did it take?

Jen: The signing up took a couple minutes.

Bob: What were the questions?

Jen: They ask you how you're generally feeling. They ask for your address and your credit card information.

Bob: Credit card? You had to pay for it, right then and there?

Jen: Right.

Bob: Did you know how much it was going to cost?

Jen: I did, because it tells you how much it's going to cost.

Bob: How much was it?

Jen: Forty-nine dollars.

Bob: Covered by insurance?

Jen: It didn't show up that it was covered by insurance.

Bob: How much was urgent care?

Jen: I don't know because I didn't go, but I expect it would have been more than that.

Bob: What happens next?

Jen: A lady comes up on a video and tells me there's going to be a provider coming soon. The video is short. Right after that, a nurse practitioner came up on the video.

Bob: Did you have video on your side too?

Jen: Yep.

Bob (*Context creates meaning*): Did you do anything to make yourself look better, or the hell with it?

Jen: I did pull my hair back but that was it. Not looking great that day.

GAME OFF

THE PHONE IS
DOWN

Think about all the anxieties that are in the way. She's never used the technology before, she doesn't even know how much it costs, or if it will even solve her problem, yet she's still going to try. Who the hell wants to learn to navigate virtual medical care for the first time while they are sick? No one! How many others want to make this progress but don't move forward?

Bob: You were sick, right? Help me, keep going.

Jen: She asked how I was doing. Gave empathy, "Sorry you don't feel good today." Then she started doing the exam by asking questions. She asked me if I could turn on the light on my phone to look down my throat. I didn't realize that I would need to have something to look down my throat.

Bob: Were there any questions where you thought, "What?"

Jen: Yeah, she asked me if I had a thermometer, which I didn't have. I told her that I felt hot. She was very nice. She made it easy.

Bob (*Contrast creates value*): Are you feeling like this is kind of cool, or are you feeling like this is weird?

Jen: I thought it was neat and fast too.

Bob (*Unpack vague words*): What does fast mean?

Jen: She went through the whole exam, asked me all the right questions, but I wasn't sitting in a waiting room; I wasn't having to drive there, I didn't have to fill out a bunch of paperwork.

Bob: You did; you had to fill out the paperwork online.

Jen: I know but it seemed easier somehow. Just the amount of time it took compared to the amount of time it would have taken to go to the doctor.

Bob (*Details, details, details*): Eight o'clock in the morning was when you decided; when did you do it?

Jen: Probably, I was on the phone with her by 8:15, and I was done by 8:25, something like that.

Bob (*Unpack vague words*): Ten minutes from the moment of signing up and logging in to being done? What does "done" mean?

Jen: She told me I had an infection and prescribed medication.

Then renewed my rescue inhaler for my asthma. And she sent it all electronically to my CVS before the call ended. I sent my husband to the pharmacy, so I didn't even have to go. I was done.

Bob: You were done; you had medicine in hand.

GAME OFF

THE PHONE IS DOWN

Listen to all that energy—the struggling and wanting to make progress but not knowing how. No wonder healthcare is so hard. Let's take a minute and capture the pushes, pulls, anxiety, and habits so we can piece this story together.

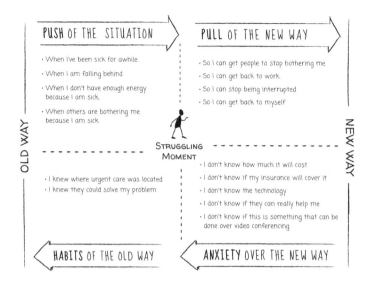

PUSH OF THE SITUATION

- When I've been sick for awhile
- When I am falling behind
- When I don't have enough energy because I am sick
- When others are bothering me because I am sick

PULL OF THE NEW WAY

- So I can get people to stop bothering me
- So I can get back to work.
- So I can stop being interrupted
- So I can get back to myself

STRUGGLING MOMENT

- I knew where urgent care was located
- I knew they could solve my problem

- I don't know how much it will cost
- I don't know if my insurance will cover it
- I don't know the technology
- I don't know if they can really help me
- I don't know if this is something that can be done over video conferencing

OLD WAY

NEW WAY

HABITS OF THE OLD WAY

ANXIETY OVER THE NEW WAY

CASE STUDY #3: CONSUMER ELECTRONICS
How Do Real Consumers Buy a Computer?

Think about the language computer companies use to sell computers: gigabytes, RAM, and CPU. Is this the way the average consumer talks when they buy a computer? Most companies tell people *how* to buy a computer. But when you talk to real consumers, *how* they bought, is completely out of sync with sales processes. How do people buy computers? Most people need help to translate the confusing features and jargon, and they are buying in spite of the way they are being sold to, not because of it. How many people want to buy a new computer but don't know how? It's a massive market. Yet companies spend fortunes competing, worrying that there are not enough consumers to go around. If they flipped the lens and focused on helping people, their market would be twice as big as everybody else's.

We interviewed Rachel, who recently bought a computer, to understand what *caused* her to buy. What language does she use when talking about buying a computer? You will see that Rachel does not buy a computer by any of the standards computer companies are selling to her. I set up the interview with Rachel as demonstrated above in the first two case studies. Let's jump right into it.

Bob: Can you tell me a little bit about yourself, your background, what you do for a living?

Rachel: I'm a freelance writer, a journalist, and I also do some work in public relations.

Bob: How long have you been writing?

Rachel: My entire career, about fifteen years.

Bob *(Setup bad questions)*: If this is too personal you don't have to answer, but are you the only income in the household?

Rachel: No, I work part-time. My husband, Eric, is the main income.

Bob: But you take it seriously? How many hours a week are you writing?

Rachel: Yes, I take it very seriously. I work about twenty to twenty-five hours a week.

Bob (*Details, details, details*): What computer did you buy?

Rachel: The Lenovo ThinkPad. I had a Mac, and I was having a lot of problems. Partially because it was older.

Bob: How old was the Mac?

Rachel: About six years old.

Bob: You had a Mac and switched to a PC? What was going on?

Rachel: I'm a contractor, and when I would interface with companies, they were all Windows-based. I had the Windows applications on the Mac, but it was glitchy. It wasn't user friendly.

Bob (*Unpack vague words*): Can you give me an example of glitchy?

Rachel: When I would incorporate Windows-based templates, they wouldn't necessarily format right.

Bob (*Contrast creates meaning*): It feels like it's a lot of extra work. Is it a little extra work or a lot of extra work?

Rachel: It was a little extra work each time but a constant issue.

Bob: What happened that made you say, "Okay, I'm done." It feels like you had work arounds.

Rachel: My daughter was admitted to the hospital. She has chronic medical issues, and it's one of the reasons I'm a contractor; I can still work while supporting her at the hospital. But I suddenly had internet issues, trouble staying connected to the hospital's server, and the battery kept dying. I wasn't always in a spot where I could plug it in while working. To make matters worse, sometimes it randomly wouldn't power on. I had deadlines to meet and now my time was very limited because I was juggling her care. I didn't have the bandwidth for computer problems!

Bob (*Contrast creates value*): Did these issues slowly ramp up over several months, or did it become a problem suddenly?

Rachel: It was a sudden problem because of my daughter's hospitalization.

Bob: Did it just die, or did you give up on it?

Rachel (*Energy matters*): I just gave up; **I'd had it!**

GAME OFF

THE PHONE IS
DOWN

There's lots of energy here. It's important that we dive into this and understand what she's "had it" with. We need to test our understanding of the energy that is pushing her to buy a new computer. Additionally, we need to understand how she figures out what to buy. Let's get into the details.

GAME ON!

THE PHONE IS
UP!

Bob: So, what happened next?

Rachel: I messaged my husband and asked him to get me a new computer ASAP.

Bob *(Context creates meaning)*: What does Eric do?

Rachel: He works in software sales. He's very technologically savvy.

Bob *(Details, details, details)*: Imagine I am shooting a documentary. Do you call him? Text him? Tell me about that conversation.

Rachel *(Energy matters)*: I texted him. It wasn't a new idea. We had talked about it several months before this happened. I had already told him that the computer was frustrating me; he suggested I get a new one. So, that day in the hospital I sent a very brief, urgent text: **"Help! I need a new computer now!"**

Bob: He was waiting for you to be frustrated enough? Did he already buy it and just have it in the package at home? Like, "Go upstairs, it's right there."

Rachel: He had already picked it out; it was in the cart online.

Bob: Let me make sure I've got the story right. For months you have several different things wrong with the computer, but the stress of now being in the hospital is the last straw. You are more pressed for time. The battery life sucks. And you decide you're done, and you need something else.

Rachel: Exactly.

Bob (*Contrast creates meaning*): Was it more about the fact that people were counting on you, or that you were frustrated.

Rachel: It was more about the fact that people were counting on me. I got nervous that I would not be able to deliver.

Bob (*Details, details, details*): What did you tell Eric you needed? Did he ask you any questions, or did he just know?

Rachel: Well, he knows what I do. I told him I needed to be able to write, seamlessly interface with Windows-based systems, video conference, and have a decent battery life.

Bob (*Unpack vague words*): Battery life, what does that mean? It's got to last eight hours, the entire day.

Rachel: No.

Bob: It was literally just boot up and be available for two hours.

Rachel: Yes.

Bob: Got it. But he didn't understand whether you needed a 350 milliampere lithium battery or an i7 processor? You didn't use that language; you were counting on him to translate?

Rachel: Yeah. And frankly, in that moment, it would have overwhelmed me if I had to figure it all out.

Bob *(Play dumb)*: Who understands all of that anyway? You've got your sick child; if you had to walk into Best Buy and figure this out, it's not going to happen, right?

Rachel *(Energy matters)*: **I would've lost it!** Thankfully, he bought it and brought it to the hospital the next day. Then he sat there with me for two hours transferring files and talking me through any differences.

GAME OFF

THE PHONE IS
DOWN

Why does it always seem that things happen at the worst time? The reality: until there's a struggling moment, an accumulation of events, people don't buy. Things will always happen at the worst time because it's that struggle that causes change. Let's debrief...

PUSH OF THE SITUATION

- When I can't count on my laptop
- When I need to create workarounds to make Windows' applications work in Macintosh
- When I have added stress because my daughter went in the hospital
- When I feel like I am falling behind

PULL OF THE NEW WAY

- So I can work in places besides my office
- So I can be more productive by not having to do the workarounds
- So I can count on the battery to work for longer periods of time
- So it will easily connect to many different Wi-Fi's
- So I can easily do video conferencing

STRUGGLING MOMENT

- How much RAM do I need?
- How much do I need to spend?
- How heavy will it be?
- Do I need special cords?
- Do I need to learn a whole new desktop?
- How am I going to transfer files?
- How am I going to figure this out?

OLD WAY

- I already have workarounds
- All my files are on the old computer

NEW WAY

HABITS OF THE OLD WAY

ANXIETY OVER THE NEW WAY

CREATING REAL GROWTH

Imagine if Chad's relationship manager had taken the time to go to his office and learn the business. Imagine how many more people might use virtual care if they weren't trying to learn about it while sick. Imagine if salespeople sold computers the way Rachel bought, talking in a recognizable language.

Most real growth does not come from stealing a small segment of customers from your competitors. It comes from truly understanding the problem your customer is trying to solve and focusing on helping them. By doing this, you reach people who wouldn't even enter the marketplace to begin with. This is where most real growth comes from—the struggling moment!

Instead, the focus of sales tends to be on the point of differentiation from competitors. One more feature: they have Bluetooth 5, we need Bluetooth 6; they have two-cell lithium ion batteries, we need three-cell. You end up over-engineering the product, until people don't even understand what they are buying. The buyer doesn't care! They want you to solve their problem; to speak their language. Salespeople should be doing these things, but they are not.

MAKING IT REAL

- On the demand-side, take a very specific struggling moment in your life and unpack the vague words you use to describe it.
- On the supply-side, unpack the most common word that people use to talk about your product or service. What does it really mean? How do you cause it?

Let's take these three case studies and begin to build a sales process around the results of our interviews that focuses on helping people make progress.

CHAPTER FIVE

MAPPING DEMAND-SIDE BUYING TO SUPPLY-SIDE SALES, MARKETING, AND CUSTOMER SUCCESS

For each of these case studies you may think there is no way anybody else lived this story. But you'd be wrong! It's not the exact details of each story that matter. Let's delve into the *why* behind Chad, Jen, and Rachel's decisions. Why did they each hire a new product or service into their lives?

- Chad switched banks, because "Bank A" failed to understand his business, treated him as a low priority, and offered him cookie-cutter options, while Chad knew there was a time pressure ahead.

- Jen tried virtual care because her coworkers kept questioning her illness; it was Sunday and she wanted to stop the probing on Monday morning.
- Rachel bought a new computer because her old one wouldn't boot; she was now pressed for time and couldn't risk missing a deadline.

Yes, the details will change, but if you conduct enough interviews you will see consistent patterns. Other people buy in similar circumstances. And for every person who bought in these circumstances, there are thousands, even millions behind them who want to make the same progress but can't figure it out. Let's look at the big picture again.

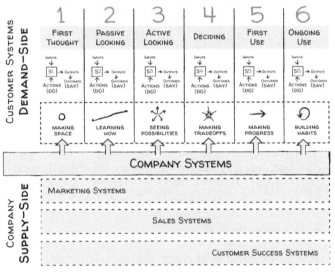

DEMAND–SIDE SALES IS ABOUT HELPING YOUR CUSTOMER MAKE PROGRESS

The key flip here is to use the timeline as the frame around how people make progress. Then take each phase of the timeline and make it a sub-system of the bigger process. By doing this, we can then look at the discrete progress people are trying to make at any point on the timeline.

- First Thought: creating space in the brain for solutions to fall into
- Passive Looking: learning, framing, and prioritizing to know what to do next
- Active Looking: seeing possibilities, framing trade-offs, and ruling things both in and out—inclusion and exclusion
- Deciding: connecting the dots into alternatives for progress, getting buy in from the group, making trade-offs, and setting expectations to measure progress
- Onboarding: first use, doing the job, and seeing both the progress and the metrics of progress achieved
- Ongoing Use: building new habits, identifying new struggling moments, and new feature development

Let's review each of the case studies and see how they connect to the supply side.

BUILDING PROGRESS ON THE BUYER'S TIMELINE

Let's take each of the three case studies and break them down into the sales framework you learned in chapter two. We'll start with the buyer's timeline and intertwine the forces at play and motivations moving the buyers along the timeline.

FIRST THOUGHT

First thought is about admitting there's a problem. "I'm not sleeping well."

How do you cause a first thought? Everything starts with understanding the customer's perspective. What are the struggling moments people have? Where do they have them? With first thought, you create questions in the buyer's mind. The questions create space in the brain for solutions to fall into. It's mostly about push. You want the buyer to question what they are doing and realize it's not working. The goal is to help people understand there could be a better way. Successfully creating a first thought means now they can see things they could not see before; they were blind but now they see. It's about opening the buyer's brain, so they are looking for a solution. Let's look at our three case studies. Where did they have their first thought?

Case Study #1: Banking

Chad's business was changing. He needed to restructure his existing debt and think about getting more money to scale the business at a different level. It became clear that "Bank A" did not understand his business; they were checking off boxes in a cookie-cutter formula.

The Question: Chad realized there was a problem, "Maybe I need a new bank?"

Case Study #2: Healthcare

Jen's willing to muscle her way through her illness but questioning colleagues make her feel self-conscious. People keep asking her, "Have you seen a doctor yet?" Some people are genuinely worried about her while others are worried about themselves. Let's be honest, no one likes to sit next to a sick coworker.

The Question: Jen's coworkers create pressure for her to solve her illness, "Maybe I should go to the doctor?"

Case Study #3: Consumer Electronics

Rachel had work arounds for the glitchy computer. Although she said there were issues for roughly a year, these problems were not enough that they triggered her first thought. Rachel's true first thought happened about six weeks before she purchased the new computer when her husband suggested she needed a new one. He injected the idea into her head, despite Rachel's defense that she did not need one.

The Question: Rachel's husband injects the thought, "Maybe I need a new computer?"

PASSIVE LOOKING

Passive looking is realizing you need to do something about the problem. "I need to find a way to sleep better."

There's very little transition between first thought and passive looking. The person is continually thinking about their problem and the question, "Maybe I can do better?" Here, you want buyers to repeatedly see your product or services popping up in their daily life, especially in places where they're struggling the most. They are exploring the possible solutions to their problem. You help them connect the dots between the question in their brain—first thought—and your solution. Now they can't stop seeing your product or service as a solution. By showing up at the right place and time, you grow their social and emotional energy around the problem. They start to think, "I need to do something," which transitions them to active looking. This is where the forces start to play a role. Let's look at our three buyers in passive looking. What did that stage look like for each buyer?

Case Study #1: Banking

Chad considers the small problems in the frame of his growing business plans. He tries to teach "Bank A" his business and they have the same conversation over and over again. Customer service is terrible; even though the business is local they will not come and sit down for a face-to-face conversation to learn the business. He raises his concerns to the bank leadership to no avail. Because he's had a first thought, Chad is continually thinking about how life would improve with a new bank.

The force—push: Chad needs to grow his business. His current bank does not understand the business and shows no interest in learning it. He needs a loan that meets his unique business needs.

The force—habit: None! "Bank A" changed relationship mangers three times without any face-to-face meetings. The new relationship manager shows no understanding of Chad's business and little interest in learning the business. The relationship has blown up.

Functional motivation: Functionally, the process with "Bank A" is arduous and shows little progress or improvement for a minimal change. They are wasting Chad's time with the exact same conversation over and over again. Chad feels like he is spinning his wheels.

Emotional motivation: Chad holds his cards close, not telling "Bank A" about the upcoming business growth plans. The relationship with this bank has become so frayed that he believes providing the full picture will make things harder. They send Chad clear signals that his business is not a priority, specifically that they are unwilling to learn the business or meet face-to-face. Overall, Chad feels like they do not have his best interests at heart. There's been a complete erosion of trust.

Social motivation: Chad does not want to seem like a "jerk," so he does not even tell "Bank A" that he is looking for another bank.

Triggering event: After the third phone call, Chad is done dealing with "Bank A." He is unwilling to keep spinning his wheels. He decides it's time to move on and begins discussing a plan with his new VP. Chad is now in active looking.

Case Study #2: Healthcare

While Jen does not go to the doctor when her coworkers initially comment, she is self-conscious about her illness now. It also starts to slow her down, and by Friday she feels behind on work. Also, on Friday her husband suggests she go to the doctor. Jen's now sorting through her medicine cabinet for over-the-counter remedies, drinking fluids, and getting plenty of rest. She passively looks all the way from Friday until Sunday. Passive looking is going through life, knowing there's a problem, and not thinking it's big enough to react yet.

The force—push: Jen does not want to go into another week at work sick. She is embarrassed by the repeated attention the illness is bringing her, and she is falling behind at her job because the illness is slowing her down.

The force—habit: She knows the urgent care option will work, but it's time consuming, and she'd have to get dressed and ready to go.

Functional motivation: After being sick on Wednesday, Thursday, and Friday, Jen feels behind at work and wants to get back to being more productive.

Emotional and social motivation: The emotional and social are tied together here. Jen feels self-conscious about coughing all day long. She does not want to stand out in this negative way.

Triggering event: Jen wakes up Sunday morning still feeling crummy. She knows that she has a long week of work ahead and decides that she should see a doctor. Jen is now in active looking.

Case Study #3: Consumer Electronics

Since her husband injected the idea of the new computer into her head, Rachel is more aware of every problem and glitch. When something goes wrong, she thinks about a new computer and the headaches it would solve. She's more aware of the pain. Suddenly Rachel's daughter is admitted to the hospital and then the computer won't even boot up.

The force—push: Rachel's under tremendous pressure and anxiety because her time is limited, and the old computer won't even boot when she needs to work.

The force—habit: Rachel has owned the Mac for six-years, it contains her files and she already has work arounds for the glitches.

Functional motivation: Rachel has deadlines to meet at work, and her time is now limited because she has the added care of her daughter.

Emotional motivation: Rachel is under tremendous emotional stress with her daughter in the hospital combined with looming work deadlines. How will she meet everyone's needs, while the computer is failing?

Social motivation: Rachel's clients are counting on her, as well as her employer.

Triggering event: The current computer won't even boot when she needs it to. This event pushes Rachel from passive to active looking. Rachel texts her husband and says she needs a new computer.

ACTIVE LOOKING

Active looking is asking yourself, "What are the alternatives for progress?"

This is where sellers can inject their possible solution to the person's problem. The mattress seller wants to introduce their mattresses at this point in the buyer's life, as a solution to a better night's sleep. If you're buying a mattress you're thinking, "It needs to keep me cool at night." "It must be soft." "Do I want foam or spring?" "How much can I afford?"

These are all independent issues. Ultimately, this is where people build their ideal solution—a target. It's important that the buyer has contrast; without contrast it becomes almost impossible to decide. The forces at play, pushes and pulls, continue to weigh on the person as they look for an ideal solution.

Case Study #1: Banking

Chad realizes he needs to actively look for another bank. He sends his VP of finance to line up meetings. They meet with four banks over a two-week time period. He gathers the different options for moving forward but he still does not tell "Bank A" that he is switching banks.

The forces—magnetism of the new solution: Two banks sit down and try to learn about Chad's business; they did not come with a preplanned presentation or a cookie-cutter formula.

The forces—anxiety of the new solution: Future growth plans put Chad in a time crunch. He knows that if he wants to switch banks, he must do so quickly.

Triggering event—the "time wall": There's the time pressure of the future acquisition pushing Chad to act quickly. He knows that if he is going to switch banks he must decide soon because he will need to repackage the entire deal.

Case Study #2: Healthcare

Jen realizes she needs to actively look for a doctor on Sunday. She considers virtual care versus urgent care because it's Sunday and her general doctor's not open. Jen wants to feel better, but it's not the real driving factor that pushes her to actively look. It's the fact that Jen knows she must go back to work the next day and everybody will question her again. Secondarily, Jen is falling behind at work. Jen never talks about feeling better as a major contributing factor.

The forces—magnetism of the new solution: Virtual care seems quick and easy on the surface. She can do it from the comfort of her couch and never even get out of her bathrobe.

The forces—anxiety of the new solution: The anxiety forces are high: "Can I work the technology?" "Can they offer an accurate diagnosis over video? "They don't have my medical records." Figuring this out for the first time while being sick is not ideal.

Triggering event—the "time wall": Jen wants to be able to return to work on Monday with a solution to tell everyone so they will back off. It's Sunday morning; the time pressure for a solution is high.

Case Study #3: Consumer Electronics

The moment the Mac fails to boot that day in the hospital,

Rachel realizes she must actively look. The event pushes her to act quickly. People are counting on her, and her time is limited because of her daughter's care. She tells her husband what she needs from a computer and insists it not be a Mac.

The force—magnetism of the new solution: There's a huge pull toward the new solution now. Rachel needs relief! The additional promise of being able to solve the smaller problems related to her Mac also create pull.

The force—anxiety of the new solution: Without the tech support her husband represents, the new solution would have high anxiety. Rachel says if she had to walk into Best Buy and figure this out in the middle of this personal crisis, she could not do it.

Triggering event—the "time wall": Rachel is under tight deadlines for work with limited bandwidth.

DECIDING

The outcome of active looking is that the buyer knows what they want. A "time wall" has pushed them into deciding. It's a trigger mechanism that forces them to choose, rather than endlessly look. Think of an hourglass, it needs to be running out of time. Without a time wall most people will not make a purchase. Now you know why mattress stores run specials every holiday. It forces people to buy. Some of these sales create false time walls because there's almost a constant sale which makes it meaningless. When deciding, people must make tradeoffs: What's most important? What's least important? This is where priorities are set, and value codes determined. It's a triangle between time, cost, and quality. No one can have it all! People set their expectations here and will base their satisfaction on the criteria they set. This is where buyers factor in bigger discounts. Interestingly, the discount is more emotional and social than financial; people want to feel good about themselves.

Case Study #1: Banking

Chad's now deciding between two banks. He started with four, but two banks arrive with preplanned presentations; immediately they are out of the running. The new banks attract Chad by listening and trying to understand Chad's business, meeting his unique needs; there's no cookie-cutter plan.

Tradeoffs: Chad decides he cares most about trust and flexibility over cost. Chad trusts the new bank because they are willing to be upfront and honest and tell him no directly rather than giving a vague maybe about what they can and can't do. Additionally, one of the contacts is a known colleague. They also provide Chad with options; they don't try to define value for Chad. Ultimately, Chad chooses flexibility over cost. It's a great example of tradeoffs. No one else gave him a more expensive option to buy ease of use. Why not? Probably because they didn't think he would take it. You do not know what your customer wants, provide contrast.

Case Study #2: Healthcare

Jen's now deciding between urgent care and virtual care. Sitting in her bathrobe on a Sunday morning, Jen contemplates her options: getting dressed and driving to the known urgent care or staying home and navigating the new technology.

Tradeoffs: Jen decides to figure out virtual care, because it's eight in the morning and she's not dressed yet. She figures that if it fails, she can always still go to urgent care.

Case Study #3: Consumer Electronics

Rachel's now deciding by setting the criteria a new computer needs to have to meet her needs. Some might think that her husband, Eric, is the one deciding, but Eric is merely acting as an advisor. It's the criteria Rachel sets forth that drives the decisions.

Tradeoffs: She insists her computer not be a Mac. She wants a good battery life and ease of use with video conferencing. Ultimately, Rachel's criteria are simple.

ONBOARDING

Acquiring a customer is about being able to onboard them and deliver in a way that matches the expectations set. You want the customer to not only feel satisfied but excited and delighted about aspects they didn't know they'd wanted or get. Delivering here is about understanding the customer upfront. The customer satisfaction should drive engineering changes. If you are not meeting expectations, what things can you improve? Most people stop selling once someone's made a purchase. But progress is about making sure you deliver on the expectations that were set. What expectations did the customer hear and did you really deliver? Nine times out of ten, dissatisfaction comes from a breakdown in communication. What are the social, emotional, and functional cues that let people understand they're satisfied or dissatisfied? The devil is always in the details; little things add up. Satisfaction, it's a bitch to accomplish. Apple spends an enormous amount of time on these details—and even they were unable to satisfy Rachel. Very few other companies spend any time on these details.

Case Study #1: Banking

Chad will base his satisfaction largely on a comparison with the old bank. If the new bank continues to treat him as a priority and understand his business, Chad will be happy.

Case Study #2: Healthcare

Jen hires virtual care. She logs onto the site and successfully completes the virtual care visit. It's easy to use and Jen never needs to leave her couch or her bathrobe. Her husband quickly picks the medication up from the pharmacy and Jen is on the path to recovery. Jen is a very satisfied customer, and likely a repeat customer; the virtual platform exceeded her expectations by being fast and easy to use.

Case Study #3: Consumer Electronics

Rachel purchases a new computer. Rachel's husband delivers the computer and helps transfer data, walking through differences. Rachel will be easy to satisfy because her comparison will be the old computer with its outdated problems.

ONGOING USE

How do you build a habit? That's the goal in ongoing use, turning the first use experience in onboarding into something that becomes a habit. You need to make it easy for consumers to use it once they've made this progress. Take consumer electronics for instance. Every update your Mac offers is about making the computer easier for you to use. Yet most people think of it as fixing bugs that you've had. So, ongoing use is about understanding different struggling moments and making the product or service better. It's about exceeding customer's expectations and addressing any struggling moments that would cause people to fire you.

Case Study #1: Banking

As Chad grows the business, he needs his bank to help him manage struggling moments. It's about a continued partnership: How is the bank going to help them when they have a cash crunch? How will it help them when they go public? What are the new future struggles of the business, and how does the bank help them overcome those struggles? What are the areas where the bank can help Chad make progress? Chad switched for one reason but he's going to stay for a whole bunch of other reasons. The bank needs to know what they are. And, it's not about pushing services Chad doesn't need; it's about understanding where the struggling moments are so the bank can offer the best services to increase their footprint inside the company.

Case Study #2: Healthcare

What other things can Jen use the virtual visit for? How does the virtual platform go from being the doctor, to the health advocate? What are those new struggling moments the consumer has, and can they use the virtual platform for it, like scheduling or for pre-visit conversations? We used the platform for scheduling future visits and created an area where consumers could log ongoing aliments for discussion in future appointments. This helped their healthcare provider be more prepared and manage their time better. Now the consumer can use the platform when they are healthy as well.

Case Study #3: Consumer Electronics

What else is Rachel going to be using her computer for over time? She bought it with the intent of using it for work but now she's noticing other features, such as the camera. What are the new struggling moments? For instance, as systems update does the computer get slower? How does the computer company make sure that the computer does not degrade in performance over time? And, are there things that Rachel could be using the computer for that she hasn't even thought of?

THE KANO MODEL

Japanese professor Dr. Noriaki Kano developed a customer satisfaction model for creating profitable products in the 1980s, which we use today in our demand-side sales approach. It's the idea that customer satisfaction is about more than the functionality of a product or service; it's also about customers' emotions. Kano breaks product attributes into three categories or needs: threshold attributes (basic), performance attributes (satisfiers), and excitement attributes (delighters). We need to talk about these things in space and time, because over time what qualifies in each category changes.

Threshold attributes are the basic features we assume a product or service contain, so we don't ask for them. In 2020, nobody buys a phone for the texting, internet, and camera. Those are all basic attributes that are assumed now but were not assumed in 2005—space and time matter.

Performance attributes are standard expectations. The more performance attributes a product or service has the more satisfied the customer. The fewer it has the more dissatisfied. If you do it, great; if you don't do it, horrible. For instance, how do websites look on my phone versus my laptop? Can I use my phone to buy and pay for items? Is it easy to share photos and documents?

Excitement attributes are unexpected things that delight the customer. When you don't do it, they don't notice or care, but when you do it, they are delighted. Right now, Facetime and features of video conferencing are exciting features as more people and businesses use them to stay connected in a personal way. Excitement features come into play when people have struggling moments that you are not responsible for and you can surprise them with a solution.

MEETING THE BUYER IN THE RIGHT TIME AND PLACE

Think of each of the six phases in the sales process as a system, like a "black box" problem in math, with inputs, outputs, and outcomes. As a salesperson, your job is to meet the buyer in each of the six stages—first thought, passive looking, active looking, deciding, and ownership—with an input. Your goal is to create an input for each of the six stages of buying, that triggers a desired output, which ultimately leads to an ideal outcome for the customer. As we start to unravel a new sales approach to meet Chad, Jen, and Rachel's needs, focus on the critical elements:

1. Find the struggling moments and understand how to solve them. People don't think about hiring and firing a product or service until they have a struggling moment. What are your customer's struggling moments? They're not what you think they are.

2. Think progress! What's the progress your customer is trying to make? Now, enable them to do THAT. It's the progress that matters, not your features and benefits.

3. Identify the tradeoffs. Don't talk features, benefits, and cost, because people are willing to make tradeoffs. What makes your product or service kick ass? Where do you say no? Basically, choose what to suck at. As Jason Fried, entrepreneur, CEO and co-founder of Basecamp says, "You're better off with a kick-ass half than a half-assed whole."

4. Understand that unfulfilled "little hires" cause "big hires."

What does that mean? The struggling moment starts in the "little hires" and if someone struggles too much they'll accumulate to a "big hire." Focus on the "little hires."

MAKING IT REAL

- On the demand-side, think about the best experience you had buying something in the last year. Why was it a great sales experience? What did they know about you that was important, that made it valuable?
- On the supply-side, think about a time when you struggled to sell your product or service. Now use the forces, motivations, and timeline to understand where you went wrong.

Next, let's connect the dots and design a plan to approach each of these buyers to help them make progress.

CHAPTER SIX

CONNECTING THE DOTS BETWEEN SALES, MARKETING, AND CUSTOMER SUPPORT

Sales, marketing, and customer support must learn to play together! Most organizations treat them as three separate entities, but they're not. And treating them as such makes sales unnecessarily hard. First thought, passive looking, and active looking are a combination of marketing and sales. Deciding, onboarding, and ongoing use are a combination of customer support and sales. Sales covers the entire process! But because the three departments don't talk, customers get mixed messages. They are bombarded with value propositions and online tactics that try to push people to decide when they are in active looking. It's making the consumer frustrated and anxious, while putting salespeople at an immediate disadvantage.

WHAT'S THE DIFFERENCE BETWEEN SALES AND MARKETING?

Marketers are the people building the brochures and advertising the product to help salespeople sell. They tend to be features driven—creating add-ons to reach the widest audience. They work at a very high, abstract, macro level. They have an ideal or imagined customer, created through the triangulation of data, such as: customer age, zip code, income level, etc. If you think about it, age and income level are not the real reason someone buys a car, but that's how marketing works—data correlation.

Sales is more complicated because it's micro-level. In sales you deal directly with the real customer. Great salespeople deal in causation not correlation. There's nothing imagined about their customer. What *causes* me to buy a car? Typically, salespeople are the highest compensated in the company. A great salesperson knows the marketing piece of the business, but also knows how to talk to people about the product, who to target, and understands why that person is driven to buy. They also ensure product delivery and must understand and manage the cashflow side of the business. Oftentimes, founders make the best salespeople because they understand the entire business inside and out.

While it sounds like sales and marketing are talking about the same thing, they're different ends of the spectrum. Macro verses micro; ideal customer versus real customer.

CASE STUDY EXAMPLES

Let's break down the three case studies by looking at the sales process as two parts instead of three.

1. Sales and marketing
2. Sales and customer support

HOW TO STOP GETTING FIRED AND START GETTING HIRED

Banks are people who sell money. How hard is it to sell money? It's not! Diligence is the only thing separating successful bankers from everybody else. Most bankers spend their time trying to assess risks and fail to understand how many people want a loan but don't apply because the process is too arduous. The market is huge, but they've made it so difficult that they're not realizing the results. Chad's experience is happening right now, today! Yet, people selling these services don't even realize it. Did Chad *want* to look for a new bank? No! Who wants to switch banks?

Chad's story is a particularly interesting case study because we can analyze it from two perspectives: the bank that got fired, and the bank that got hired.

Sales and Marketing

Let's start from the first thought, and from a sales and marketing perspective. Imagine you are the competing bank. How would you attract Chad? How would you package something with the right message, features, and advertising to pull him in? Remember that the push of the situation and the magnetism of the new solution need to be stronger than the anxieties and habit before someone will buy. Many people think all banks are the same. So if you think this, and your bank sucks, you don't say, "Oh boy, I think I need to get a better bank." You don't believe there is a better bank. As a result, you don't even know that you're struggling with your current bank. Part of marketing and selling is showing customers that something else exists.

When people have a first thought and begin passively looking, it's about being in the right place at the right time. To that end, if we were bankers trying to attract this type of business, we'd start with a "Lunch and Learn" to connect businesses together and build a network. It's also a great way to get your existing clients to talk about you to prospective clients. The conversation should not be about loans and terms, it should focus on the progress people are trying to make: What could you be doing if you had more money? How would your business grow if you had access to better capital? Then try to understand their anxieties: What's holding you back? How can we help you mitigate the risk? How can you prepare for the downside? No one knows where the economy is going, but who's by your side to help you figure it out?

When somebody transitions to active looking and asks for a quote say, "I need thirty minutes to an hour of your time to understand your business before I can give you a quote." In that meeting set the expectations, "I'll come back with three alternatives that will help you frame your situation better. From there we will morph a fourth option by merging the best of three. If at any point you reach out and I am not available, I will contact you within twenty-four hours." Then set the tone, "I'm a straight shooter. If it's a no, I'll tell you no; if it's a yes, I'll tell you yes." By setting the expectations up front, you're already ahead of the competition.

Let's contrast this to what most banks do: "Let me tell you about who we are..." then they name drop their clients and offer a wide menu of options. You're not a banker, it's confusing. They don't understand your business or know you. And you don't care who they represent.

But when you sell from the demand-side and understand their progress and struggles first, you're ahead of the game. You take the time to learn the business. You educate them on their options, specific to their needs only. At this point, you've built trust; now you realize that trust is caused. You've changed the way you sell loans.

THE JEWELER EFFECT

When the diamond industry came up with the notion of cut, clarity, and color to help people shop for diamonds, jewelers were completely against it. They felt it would ruin their relationship with customers and undermine what they did. The opposite happened. It educated consumers because now they could make tradeoffs. They could buy a bigger diamond at a lower price, by sacrificing color or clarity and vice versa. Diamond sales grew almost ten times as a direct result, and jewelers who were willing to educate customers got ninety percent of the sales. It was ultimately about trust!

Sales and Customer Support

Now think about the old bank, "Bank A," that got fired: What could they have done differently? What would you have changed about the situation? What messaging and interactions, could have stopped this from happening?

It all starts with customer support. Most sales models think of new business as harder to get than renewals, therefore, they put their lower-level people on renewals. But renewals are just as hard, sometimes riskier, than new business because you've got history to overcome or reshape. The "big hire" on the timeline is the beginning, not the end. "Bank A" failed to recognize this and took the customer for granted; as a result there's zero force of habit in the relationship. What changes should "Bank A" make to retain their customers?

First, "Bank A" needs an onboarding process that enables their sales representatives to help the customer. A simple change in the way they handoff accounts from one relationship manager to another would have made a big difference here. The first meeting should be face-to-face, to learn about their business. They should teach their people to be curious about their customer's business.

Second, they should establish regular, meaningful wellness visits with their customers where they ask pointed questions and offer real assistance: Where is the business going next year? What big projects do you have? Now, they should come back with ways to help them save money or have access to something new: Can they connect the customer to a helpful resource? Can they offer a new loan that would provide savings? "Bank A" needs to find ways to stay engaged with their customers. If they do this, renewals will become easy.

Finally, "Bank A" needs to listen and be honest. If you hear trust decay repeatedly, it's a vulnerability. They built trust initially; they got the deal. But then they made changes and eroded the trust. They need to do a trust check, and let's be clear, customers will lie to you if you simply ask, "Do you trust us today?" That's a terrible question, dig deeper. The policy should always be to answer questions in an upfront and honest way, never string people along. If the answer's no, say no. Most salespeople try to never say no, but that's a bad approach. They should assemble their house of cards on trust.

Remember, the most vulnerable people in your portfolio are your current clients because you've learned to ignore them.

UNDERSTANDING HOW PEOPLE CHOOSE A HEALTHCARE PROVIDER

We were hired in this instance by a healthcare company that was starting to build urgent cares, but also had a virtual care platform and general practices. They initially wanted to know what causes people in non-emergency situations to choose urgent care. So, we set out to interview people about their choices over the last few months. What circumstances led them to choose urgent care, virtual care, or their general doctor? Think of it this way, we have email, texts, and phone calls. When do you use each? How do you decide to pick up the phone and call somebody versus texting them? We have all these codes in our head that tell us when to do each and everyone's codes are different. We want to learn people's codes for choosing to engage in healthcare and how they decided on the provider. What made this the right choice at this time? We're trying to frame the situations people are in when they are trying to make progress, so we can help them.

Sales and Marketing

Jen was one of dozens of patients interviewed about her health care choices. Immediately, it became clear that the anxiety factor for all our interviewees was high. Remember, value is created and money is made by solving the anxiety side of the equation. And Jen's interview, along with many others, netted us great feedback for the virtual side of the business. In hindsight it's obvious, nobody wants to learn new technology while sick, but it was an a-ha moment. At the time, around 2015, people were not doing Zoom and other virtual conferencing nearly as much—a foreign concept. Why in the world are we asking patients to learn new technology when they feel their worst? Ridiculous!

After this insight we asked ourselves: how do we introduce them to the virtual visits sooner? Because this client owned the virtual care platform, as well as urgent care and general practices, we decided to leverage the entire system. They began by introducing the virtual platform at wellness visits, which acted as a first thought trigger. As patients were leaving, they helped them navigate the platform by asking them to set up next year's appointment on it with help. Patients could push a button and a physician assistant would appear. As patients concluded the scheduling call, the medical provider reminded them they could do this anytime they needed medical help. Additionally, every time someone called for an appointment, providers encouraged them to schedule through the virtual visit platform. The patient learned to make the technology work while they were well. It quadrupled the virtual visits.

Now that patients knew how to use the virtual platform, the medical provider targeted patients with billboard ads explaining when patients could use virtual care. The original ads simply explained that virtual visits were available 24/7. The new ads targeted people in that moment where they were passively looking: "Feeling sick? Don't put your plans on hold, stay productive." People knew how to use the platform now and realized they only needed a fifteen-minute window between meetings, instead of getting in their car, driving to the doctor, waiting, etc. The provider also ran billboard ads that explained when you could use virtual care, such as when you're sick, fighting allergies, and so on, because our interviews revealed people were unsure. Context creates value!

Sales and Customer Support

From these interviews the medical provider found there were three different contexts which led someone to potentially choose urgent care. First, the patient felt sick, but their overall medical history was complicated: diabetes, heart condition, or another chronic illness. They were afraid to go to the urgent care, because they didn't have their medical records. This anxiety caused them to delay care out of fear that they'd forget to explain critical aspects of their health to the new provider. Second were patients who felt sick; however, they knew what was wrong because they'd had it before—a sinus infection or a urinary tract infection. They wanted quick, no nonsense care. Third, something's wrong, but it's not major. They cannot self-diagnose, and they want answers. This patient is mostly seeking quick reassurance.

The medical provider revamped their process to help these people as well. First, they began sending emails to patients and their regular care doctors right after appointments. This gave patients the confidence that nothing would be missed. The provider found that the force of habit was not very high, and most people did not like their doctor. So, if they could ease the patient's anxiety about a lack of connection to their medical records, they'd hire us. Second, the provider created an incoming form to help triage patients. They asked them five questions: Have you had this before? Do you know what it is? Do you have any other complications? And do you have your medical records within our system?

Originally, each patient was supposed to spend eighteen minutes with a doctor. This form got most people down to five minutes, while increasing satisfaction from 28 percent to 78 percent. Patients who came into urgent care after we implemented the changes had a propensity to come back four times as often as they did prior to the new system. We effectively changed the way we onboarded new patients by optimizing the entire system around solving their anxieties and meeting their personal progress. Instead of just marketing to them more, we were able to set expectations better and get people to use urgent care more often.

By focusing on urgent care during the interview, we found other areas to improve business, such as the medical provider's virtual platform. As you can see, we did not steer Jen's interview to focus on urgent care despite that being the client's focus. By understanding Jen and other patients' not choosing their service, we learned valuable information.

HOW TO SYNCH SELLING COMPUTERS TO THE WAY PEOPLE BUY

The way Rachel bought a computer is not in sync with the way computer companies sell them. Computer companies don't think about the way people buy. Instead they market by screen size, processing speed, and RAM. They never talk about how to solve a customer's struggling moment. Selling computers is not about selling computers; it's about helping people make progress with fitting a computer into their lives. Rachel wanted simple assurances: Will it power up? Will it interface with various formats? Will the video conferencing be seamless? Will it have all the latest programs for a professional writer? But she needed a translator to get those answers—most people do.

Sales and Marketing

Triggering a first thought is about helping people recognize that a problem already exists. Computer companies should be talking about your current computer's problems: What bothers you the most? What are you frustrated about? If you had a new computer, what would be better? Computer marketing should be saying, "Life can be better! Imagine if you didn't have to deal with these problems." Remember, people are not paying attention until they see the problem in their own lives. Computer companies should be highlighting your struggle to be even greater than you perceive it. And this push force should become bigger as people move into passive looking.

Based on Rachel's context, we need to figure out where people are pressed for time and market there: hospitals, kid's sporting events, stadiums, etc. Anyplace where you're waiting, trying to work, and lack access to a plug. Remember, Rachel had computer problems for months before she acted. She needed an event to push her from passive looking to active looking. In June she was not ready to buy a computer because there was no pressure. She had more time and access to a plug. But it's that moment of pressure, when it's logistically challenging to buy, that she was the most receptive. Rachel was tolerant for nine months, she had a functional problem, but emotionally she couldn't do it yet.

To get people from passive to active looking you need an event, natural or artificial. This event needs to make buyers, like Rachel, painfully aware of how much they are doing to compensate for their computer's deficits. As a salesperson, you might watch Rachel navigate her computer and ask questions: Why do you do this? Why did you do that? How many times has your computer stopped working? The questions alone will trigger the thought, "Yeah, why am I doing all this?" Several months before Rachel purchased her computer, she could have been nudged to active looking with the right questions: what are you going to do if it doesn't boot back up? By putting the doubt in her mind, it creates the space for her to think, "I've got to create a plan. I don't want to be caught off guard."

Now Rachel's in active looking. When people are in active looking, they think of every possibility. But the options are not connected to each other, they are separate and independent. They are deciding between a bigger screen vs. a smaller screen, but they don't understand the difference between the two beyond size. Is the bigger screen heavier? Does it affect battery life? They don't understand the tradeoffs. It's just about features and possibilities. Active looking is accumulating facts, but they don't have enough information to decide.

There's a big disconnect between Rachel's requirements and computer companies. For instance, Rachel needed a reasonably better battery life. Now engineers are arguing if it's four hours, six hours, or eight. They get so myopic on the little things that they fail to understand the struggle. Rachel just wants a computer that turns on and lasts through a two-hour video conference call when she does not have access to a power outlet. Her expectations are very low.

Rachel's criteria was more about getting the replacement fast than perfection. Emotionally, she's extremely stressed, she's got no time, she needs a good enough replacement and needs it in under twenty-four hours. The criteria she gave her husband had nothing to do with the biggest screen or any of the other features that computer companies advertise on. She bought it to be up and running in twenty-four hours. She was willing to make tradeoffs to get it up and running quickly. She didn't want to wait two weeks for the best computer; she wanted good enough tomorrow.

Sales and Customer Support

The key is to help consumers make tradeoffs. Rachel's husband made the tradeoffs for her. People will pay an additional 10 percent of the value of the computer for the service that Rachel's husband offered. For someone to just tell them what they need and to produce it with a money back guarantee. Most people would rather pay someone to be accountable, because then if there's a problem they can take it back easily. You can't buy a computer this way; nobody sells them this way!

Computer companies need to talk to Rachel the way her husband does, understand her problem, and help her solve it by introducing solutions in a language that makes sense. Skip the features and benefits, ask her the problem she is trying to solve, and deliver a computer in twenty-four hours that solves that problem. Then spend thirty minutes walking her through any questions. As a salesperson, you need to help get Rachel the best computer to solve her problem, and the best computer for Rachel is not the best computer for everybody. The customer should define the way a product is being sold, rather than the company dictating the way a customer buys, but that's often not the case. They need to understand how the customer wants to buy.

While Rachel seems to be in a unique time and place, this space in time repeats itself a thousand times a day, every day, somewhere else in the world. Maybe the struggle is not specifically the same, but it boils down to the same place.

MAKING IT REAL

- On the demand-side, think about the last time you had a bad sales experience. Why was it so bad?
- On the supply-side, think about the last three sales you made. Why did they work or not work?

Sales no longer feels icky, because it's about helping people make progress on their terms. Sales is now progress.

CHAPTER SEVEN

MOVING FROM PUSHING PRODUCTS TO CREATING PULL FOR PROGRESS

Why do people buy a Snickers? Why do people buy a Milky Way? Traditional supply-side thinking says that Snickers and Milky Way compete for the same customers. After all, they sit side-by-side in the candy aisle and are made with similar ingredients.

But what motivates someone to buy a Snickers instead of a Milky Way? It turns out that people buy a Snickers because they are running out of energy; they need a boost. Their stomach is growling, and Snickers feels like food—the nougat, caramel, and peanuts form a ball, it's hard. Snickers does not compete with Milky Way at all. It competes with a sandwich, Red Bull, and a cup of coffee. Whereas, Milky Way slides down your throat, coating your mouth with chocolate and endorphins. It's a candy bar. People usually eat it alone, after an emotional event, good or bad, and it helps them feel better or acts as a reward. Milky Way competes with ice cream, brownies, and a glass of wine.

Understanding this dynamic was a game changer for Snickers. They flipped the lens on sales and launched a commercial that spoke to people in this specific moment in time. The advertisement opened on a field with a group of young men playing football with Betty White. Betty's struggling, everyone's yelling at her. Then someone hands her a Snickers bar, she takes a bite and transforms back into himself—another one of the young men playing football. "You're not YOU when you're hungry," the narrator says. "Snickers satisfies!"

This ad took Snickers to over $3.5 billion in less than ten years. And it's a perfect example of demand-side sales. When Snickers reframed their product from competing with Milky Way—supply-side selling—to solving the customer's struggling moment—demand-side selling—they created pull for their product by helping people make progress.

Today most sales still operate under a supply-side model. Industry disruptors like Casper, SNHU, and our personal experiences with over 3,500 products and services are still not the norm.

WHAT'S WRONG IN SALES TODAY?

Unfortunately, most salespeople are not taught to think of themselves as a helper. They are taught to think about their product, the what, with all its features and benefits, and the people, the who, as a set of demographics. But they're missing the five W's and two H's—who, what, when, where, why, how, and how much. Salespeople have been trained to only focus on a small portion of the equation. In fact, it seems many salespeople are operating under the marketing framework.

The problem goes back to the 1985 sale of Nabisco we spoke about in the introduction. When brand equity became more valuable than cashflow, marketers took the lead. It's a fundamental powershift that's relegated salespeople to order takers, not helping to generate demand. Marketers are expected to create demand, and sales is to follow the leads generated. It's a flawed approach that sets salespeople up to fail. Demand is only generated by a customer's struggling moment. If there is no struggle, there is no demand.

Additionally, other disciplines have developed major frameworks, theories, and tools to help them do what they do. In marketing they have brand equity, features, benefits, and a whole set of tools wrapped around how to market. But from a sales perspective all you get are leads. Salespeople need frameworks, theories, and tools to help them as well. Sales and marketing are not one and the same.

It's the lack of resources that's turned traditional supply-side sales into an icky business. Salespeople are put under tremendous pressure, everything they do is viewed through the lens of the product and profit. The focus is on the "church of finance," where cashflow is king and budget forecasting is center stage to keep banks and investors happy. When the "church of finance" is driving decisions, they're not made in the customer's best interest. As a result, salespeople end up promoting and creating endless ways in which to push people to buy their product or service before they're ready. The reality is the push mentality does more harm than good—failed expectations and buyer's remorse.

It's easy to negatively judge sales from the outside, but sales is hard. Great salespeople know a lot. They have what we call horizontal skills, meaning their knowledge crosses every department of the company. Salespeople are one of the few people in the entire organization who know everything. They are close to the CEO in knowledge but on the frontline. They are marketers who know the people and know the product at the same time. We call marketers 'a salesperson who can't close,' because they don't have the same in-depth knowledge that great salespeople must have. They work in features and benefits, while sales pushes beyond this, helping to reduce anxieties. Great salespeople deal in causation, not correlation. They need to understand the real customers, not an imagined, personified version. It's that micro level of understanding that makes sales so tremendously hard.

"THE MAN IN THE RING"

In April 1910, former United States President Theodore Roosevelt gave one of his most widely quoted speeches about critics:

"It is not the critic who counts; not the man who points out how the strong man stumbles, or where the doer of deeds could have done them better. The credit belongs to the man who is actually in the arena, whose face is marred by dust and sweat and blood; who strives valiantly; who errs, who comes short again and again, because there is no effort without error and shortcoming; but who does actually strive to do the deeds; who knows great enthusiasms, the great devotions; who spends himself in a worthy cause; who at the best knows in the end the triumph of high achievement, and who at the worst, if he fails, at least fails while daring greatly, so that his place shall never be with those cold and timid souls who neither know victory nor defeat."

It's easy to judge sales from the outside, to hold a derogatory view. But, people on the outside don't truly understand the pressures on the inside: trying to close deals, knowing everything and anything. Salespeople are on the inside of the ring, and it's a tremendously hard job with few tools and resources.

REFRAMING SELLING AS SERVING

If you're struggling to be great at sales, you're not alone. While seasoned salespeople already instinctively understand the concepts taught here, they had to muddle their way through the ick at first too. We wrote this book so you don't have to struggle like I did all those years ago selling kitchen countertops. It's our hack for becoming a seasoned salesperson without failing for twenty years first.

Now that you've flipped the lens, what does sales look like under the demand-side paradigm? Not sales! Sales turns into serving and helping others. You see the world through your customer's eyes. You're no longer a salesperson but an advisor, coach, or helper. The role of the salesperson in a demand-side sales approach is to assist customers in shaping and framing their progress. Salespeople are the shepherds that help customers go down the path of progress. When you approach sales as a guide, assisting customers, you stop pushing your product by adding endless features and benefits, and create pull instead by framing the context, outcomes, and tradeoffs for the customer. People need someone to help them navigate their way to make progress. The salesperson's job is to help customers figure out what the options are by first understanding what's important to them.

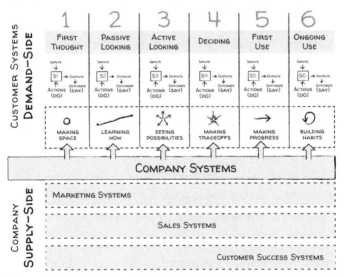

DEMAND-SIDE SALES IS ABOUT HELPING YOUR CUSTOMER MAKE PROGRESS

Let's review the six stages of buying one more time.

- First Thought: creating space in the brain for solutions to fall into
- Passive Looking: learning, framing, and prioritizing to know what to do next
- Active Looking: seeing possibilities, framing trade-offs, and ruling things both in and out—inclusion and exclusion
- Deciding: connecting the dots into alternatives for progress, getting buy in from the group, making trade-offs, and setting expectations to measure progress
- Onboarding: first use, doing the job, and seeing both the progress and the metrics of progress achieved
- Ongoing Use: building new habits, identifying new struggling moments, and new feature development

A SNAPSHOT OF DEMAND-SIDE SALES

Let's look at the six stages of the buying process once more from the perspective of a car salesperson. As we do, think of it as a system for making progress. What would someone do to avoid the cliché of becoming the icky, used car salesperson? How would they transform the process to become a helper?

First Thought

Start in system one, first thought. The customer becomes aware of the problem: "My car just went into the shop to get serviced; it's got 110,000 miles on it." At this moment they wonder, "Maybe I'm ready for a new car." This is the first thought. The buyer is realizing their car is going to need a few fixes. So, what should the salesperson do to help them think through their decision? First, they should frame the situation in a way that helps the customer understand what it will look like if they keep their old car: "After we've done these repairs, here's the next adjustments you can expect, and the estimated costs." Providing this information creates pushes.

Passive Looking

Now, it's a great time to offer them a complimentary loaner; their car's in the shop after all. So, for two days while the old car is serviced, they drive around in a brand-new car. Suddenly, they realize what life would be like if they upgraded now. It's passive looking at its best. They're not looking for a car, they're not asking for a test drive, but while their car is serviced, they're learning what's possible. No one's pushed them. Additionally, up until this moment, it's come through a trusted advisor, a serviceperson they've known, ideally, for years. With zero push, you're helping them figure out whether they need a new car by framing the situation they're in and showing them what's possible.

When they return, the service person should reiterate what's next for the old car: "Here's what your next service interval looks like, and here's the things you can expect between now and 150,000 miles." This creates more push. The buyer is thinking, "Do I really want to spend $5,000 more on this car?" Now's a good time for the salesperson to step in and follow up: "Well, if you have any interest, I can get your car appraised. Let you know how much it's worth. It could be a good down payment for a new car."

Active Looking

The moment they agree to the appraisal, they're in active looking. Active looking is about shaping up their options: "Where do I drive? How far do I go? What kind of car do I want to have? How long will I keep it? Do I want to buy something smaller? Do I want to buy the same type of car?" Think of active looking as going deeper. The buyer is trying to figure out how this is going to fit into their life. As the salesperson you should be asking questions to frame out their definition of value. Then it's about getting a few products and comparing.

This is where contrast to create meaning is extremely important! They might think they want a Ford instead of an Audi, or maybe they want an SUV instead of a minivan. Your job as a salesperson is to give them contrasting options so they can frame out what they value. If they want that SUV, show them an oversized SUV, a small sized SUV, and the minivan. If they want the Ford fully loaded show them that it's about the same price as the Lincoln loaded. But also show them the Audi, it's only a little bit more expensive and if they buy it slightly used, it's in the same price range.

There's a book called *Predictably Irrational* by Dan Ariely, which speaks to the concept of contrast and options. It's the notion that if you give people three choices, the first thing they'll do is eliminate one of the three. Then, once they've eliminated one, they will compare the other two to the one they eliminated. Interestingly, they now have two reference points for what's in and what's out. However, when you give somebody two things, they struggle to decide. And if you give them one thing, they typically can't choose. So, in sales when someone is deciding, it's important to have enough contrast to create meanings. Otherwise, they cannot make the tradeoffs they need to make for progress.

Deciding

After providing them contrasting options, you may find that they originally had no intention of buying the Audi, but when they realize the one-year-old Audi is the same price, their thinking changes. The competitive sets for buyers are very different than what the people in the car industry think they are. They don't imagine the Ford and Audi competing, because they only think in terms of new versus new. A great salesperson understands this dynamic and helps frame these tradeoffs.

Now they are in system four, deciding. For the buyer to move from deciding to ownership there needs to be a time wall, a pressure cooker that forces them to make tradeoffs, like a sale. It's the moment of truth, where people make decisions, and in this moment the context changes or magnifies. It's very different than active looking. It's like the trash compactor in *Star Wars*; when things get closer, they're willing to think differently and give up on certain things. Partly, it's the time wall. As you approach the time wall it distorts everything so people can make tradeoffs.

Onboarding and Ongoing Use

Here is where value, satisfaction, and expectations are locked in. Here's where people make a commitment. The key is the word "commitment" versus "transaction," because there are exceptions where people are committed to doing something, but they are not able to follow through. The moment that they've committed is where all the expectations are locked in. Whatever they thought was going to happen before is reframed, and almost poured in concrete, when they commit.

A bad salesperson doesn't set clear expectations. Setting clear expectations is all about understanding value from the customer's perspective. What do they value? And when discussing value, you'll often find people expect discounts. They think, "Well, I don't need that feature, so I should get some money back." This is about understanding what the customer values and only talking in those terms. If they complain about cold seats, talk about that feature, but if they live in a hot climate, don't even bring it up. You should not be talking about every feature and benefit of each car, only the ones applicable to their specific definition of value.

The moment they commit, buyers adjust their reference point of what better means. Better doesn't mean better than everything they've looked at. It means better than the old product they fired—their old car. People think of better in the competitive set, but that's not right. It's better than the old reference point. The concept of better is important, because of the anxiety forces at play. If they are not addressed, there's buyer's remorse. Buyer's remorse comes from two things: A buyer didn't think through all the criteria. Or, they were not able to see the full picture until after they bought. When you understand your buyer, as demand-side sales teaches, you anticipate their problems and solve them before they even realize they exist.

Demand-side sales is like having night vision goggles. People think sales is just a numbers game of percentages and probability. If you bring in enough people, cars will sell. They're not taking the time to understand *why* people buy. They don't ask questions: What do you like? What don't you like? Why are you buying a new car? They don't talk about car loans. If they were paying attention, they'd help. They'd know the customer's requirements, show them contrasting options, and frame their tradeoffs. They'd help them frame it out then use a time wall to force a decision. When you do this, selling becomes serving.

HELPING PEOPLE MAKE PROGRESS

As we come full circle, we want you to think of the best sales-person you've ever had, whether you were buying a car or make-up. You probably didn't think of them as a salesperson at the time of purchase. "Oh yeah, Joe helped me buy my car. But Joe's not really a salesman; he's like a concierge." You don't want to call Joe a salesperson, because it's so derogatory. Supply-side selling caused this dynamic. We hope we've changed the way you view the words *sales* and *selling*.

Demand-side sales is about pulling people toward progress. Flipping this lens flips the role of salesperson from icky used car salesperson to a helper. When you get away from push-ing your product, you start to make people feel like you're helping them; you're their concierge. You're no longer the used car salesperson. A great salesperson listens first and then helps.

MAKING IT REAL

- On the demand-side, think about something that you are considering buying and map out where you are using the framework. Can you identify some of your own behavior and map it to the timeline? Now use this information to help yourself make progress.
- On the supply-side, look at something you are trying to sell, such as convincing your significant other to go on vacation or buy a new mattress. Now flip your perspective to their

world. Where are they on the timeline? What progress are they trying to make?

Let's take one last look at the key points outlined throughout *Demand-Side Sales 101*.

CONCLUSION

The very foundation of demand-side sales is being helpful, empowering, curious, and creative; you must understand *why* people do what they do. Once you truly master demand-side sales, it's like riding a bike. But, also like riding a bike, you only truly learn it by doing it—practice, practice, practice. Let's wrap-up *Demand-Side Sales 101* with a summary of the three main principles for success, the three main myths we are trying to dispel, and the best ways to get started. We feel like we fed you with a firehose, so let's boil it down.

THE THREE PRINCIPLES FOR SUCCESS

- **Principle #1: People buy for their own reasons.** It's more about progress than about your product or service. Your job as a salesperson is to help people make progress on their terms; it's about more than selling and making the "almighty dollar." Approaching sales from this mindset will set you apart as a great salesperson.

- **Principle #2: Nothing is random; everything is caused.** Understanding the causal mechanisms of *why* people do what they do, down to the action level, is critical. It will help you see patterns and sell better while helping people make progress faster.
- **Principle #3 The struggle creates demand.** The struggling moment is the seed for all sales. Where do people struggle? Helping people make progress is embedded in finding these struggling moments. So, find the struggling moment!

THE THREE MYTHS TO DISPEL

- **Myth #1: Supply creates demand; build it and they will buy it.** No, the product does not create demand. However well-meaning your aspirations, they are not enough to sell your product and cause people to make the necessary tradeoffs. People want to be their definition of best, not yours. It's about fitting your product into their life by understanding the progress they are trying to make.
- **Myth #2: Sales are random, the needle in a haystack mentality.** This is the idea that you just need to find people and they will buy. Sales is not about finding people; it's about creating demand. Many salespeople operate under the probability framework: "If I get my product in front of enough people eventually it will sell. I've got to play the numbers." Random is one of the worst concepts in the

world, it causes people to wait and work harder in vain. Sales are caused; you must build a system.

- **Myth #3: Sales is about convincing people, and you can convince anyone to do anything.** Salespeople don't convince people to buy, people convince themselves. They buy for their own reasons. The customer defines the value. You need understand them first, and then your product and how it fits into their lives.

WHERE TO START?

1. **Look at your own buying habits.** Think of something you purchased recently that took you a long time to finally buy. Now, sit down with a friend or family member and talk about *how* and *why* you purchased it. It doesn't matter if it's a car, phone, or a meal service. Whatever it is, try to uncover what happened, and don't do it alone. Dig deep into yourself and understand the social, emotional, and functional reasons *why* you did what you did. Understand *how* you bought. You will realize that the irrational becomes rational with context. It's ultimately a low-risk way to practice this new approach before applying it to your product or service.

2. **Practice helping your friends and family.** Question them about something they bought recently. This is a great way to practice the interrogation techniques from chapter four. Walk through whatever they bought and try to understand *how* and *why* they did what they did. You

can also use this approach with your kids. Understand the struggling moments that caused them to say, "I need help in homework," or "I'm not good at this sport." Now use the techniques you learned to help them make progress. See if you can sell your child on a new path.

3. **Now that you're comfortable, start applying the demand-side sales approach to your customer.** First, talk to someone who recently bought your product or service and made progress with it. Now have a conversation and figure out what caused them to say, "Today's the day I'm going to buy..." What was going on in their life? Second, think of your next presentation or PowerPoint as helping somebody make progress. Can you design your presentation to help people see their context and desired outcome? Can you address their anxieties, and understand their tradeoffs? Most presentations are designed from the functional perspective, but not the emotional and social perspectives. Can you design a presentation aimed at all three motivations?

Now take each of these three starting points and apply the knowledge you've learned throughout *Demand-Side Sales 101*.

1. Articulate the buyer's timeline and the four forces of progress. Do you understand the dominoes that had to fall before the sale happened?

2. Summarize it into a meaningful story, including the functional, emotional, and social motivations.

3. Design a sales process to help others make progress.

Finally, there are a few great books we recommend that will serve to propel your demand-side sales skills forward.

Never Split the Difference by Chris Voss. He's a CIA negotiator and teaches techniques for becoming a better investigator with tips for how to uncover the causal mechanisms behind why people do what they do. It's the ultimate guide to interviewing.

To Sell Is Human by Daniel Pink. He believes everyone is in sales, to one degree or another, and he explores the social sciences behind great sales. He believes there are fundamental attributes to great salespeople—"glass half-full" types.

The Sandler Rules by David Mattson. It's a great foundational approach to learning the language of sales.

The Seven Habits of Highly Effective People by Stephen Covey. It's a manual for improving both professionally and personally and is very applicable to demand-side sales.

The Little Red Book of Selling by Jeffrey Gitomer. It's a pocket-reference guide for learning to sell yourself with twelve and a half principles.

TRANSFORMING SELLING AND BUYING

We hope the words *sales* and *selling* have undergone a metamorphosis in your mind, like watching *The Wizard of Oz* in black and white versus color. It all seemed so simple and plain at first, but now you've got color and texture. When you frame sales around the lens of helping people make progress, on their terms, it's no longer a negative. You're creating value!

Sales is the lifeblood of any organization, but more than that, it's everywhere, and in everything that you do. Beyond making you better at sales, we hope this book helps you in life, by not only changing the way you sell, but by changing the way that you buy. We hope you become more purposeful and understand *why*. It's liberating to know that the only person standing in the way of your personal progress is YOU. And, you don't need four years to decide how to buy a car, phone, or whatever else you've failed to make progress with. Now, you'll understand *why* you've failed to make progress and be able to move forward. Your purchases as a result will become more purposeful and less wasteful.

Demand-side sales is about listening more intently and understanding other people's perspectives. These are more than sales skills; they are life skills as well. It's our hope that this book will lead to deep and meaningful conversations with your friends, family, and customers, so that you can help everybody around you make progress.

APPENDIX

THE TOP FIVE TOOLS FOR SERVING CUSTOMERS

Now that you understand demand-side sales, this appendix will serve as a cheat sheet, or back-pocket reference guide, for moving forward. At this point, you've already interviewed past customers and understand the progress they made with your product or services. But how do you approach new customers and apply that progress? We call these best tips from throughout the book "progress tools" and we've put them in one handy reference guide. These are forward-looking tools that will help you approach new customers and apply your knowledge.

PROGRESS TOOLS

1. FRAMING THE PROBLEM

This starts with framing out the struggling moment and understanding the context and outcomes the customer is seeking. Think of these as questions you want to ask in order to help someone make progress. These questions can be divided into push, pull, anxieties, and habit.

Push Questions: What are you struggling with? What's not happening that you want to happen? Where's your frustration? Why are you doing this now? What don't you like about your current product or service?

Pull Questions: What are you hoping for? What's going to be different once you've got something new in your life?

Anxiety Questions: What are you worried about? What's your greatest concern about getting rid of the old product or service? What's your greatest concern about putting something new into your life? How's that going to impact everybody else around you? What are they going to say?

Habit Questions: Even though there are problems, what do you love the most about your current product or service? What are you willing to give up in order to get something better? What are you not willing to give up?

These are very standard questions that can frame a buyer's situation so that you quickly understand where they are and why they're doing what they're doing. This is where you want to think about the social, emotional, and functional motivations. Finally, understand the buyer's time wall.

Time Wall Questions: When do you need to make this decision by? Why then?

2. UNPACKING LANGUAGE

This goes back to unpacking vague words and concepts, such as easy, convenient, fast, healthy, etc.

Unpacking Questions: What does THAT (insert: easy, convenient, fast, healthy) mean? Tell me what THAT is? Tell me what THAT is not. Give me an example of THAT. Give me an example of not THAT. Ultimately, it's asking questions down to actions. For example...

Customer: Well, it's easy.

You: Easy like what?

Customer: It's easy like a car.

You: In what way is it easy like a car?

Customer: It's a known process. You open the door, put the

key in the ignition, etc. There are steps but you know exactly what to do. It's familiar and easy.

You: But those steps weren't always familiar and easy. At the beginning you had to learn them.

Customer: Yeah, but I could learn it.

You: Ah, so easy is about being able to learn it and repeat it. Got it. Give me an example of something that's not easy.

Customer: Docking a boat. I don't do it often enough. I know the procedures, but it's hard to do. And it varies so much on the weather conditions. So, I can't do it consistently.

Unpacking is about getting down to the action. It's asking "why" five times, not literally five times, but it's peeling back the onion. The other part about unpacking is finding the reference point. Let's say you are talking in terms of healthy. Kale chips are healthy but wanting to be healthy and eating kale chips are not synonymous. When you start to unpack it, you realize it's just got to be healthier than Doritos and Cheetos—something like SunChips. I can build a $400 million product based off that, but I can't build a $400 million kale chip business because they suck. So, with unpacking it's never healthy, fast, or easy. It's always healthier, faster, easier than the reference point. You need that reference point.

3. PROTOTYPING TO LEARN

Prototyping is "let's pretend." Once you have the context and the outcomes framed you want to pull in contrasting solutions to their problem.

For instance, let's say you are a real estate agent selling houses. You want to initially show the buyer three very different houses. Even if they already told you that they don't want a rancher, you take them there to understand their value code better. Once at the rancher, ask them to tell you three things they like, and three things they don't. The contrast will help you understand their value code, not change their mind about ranchers. You might learn that they like having the bedrooms close together, or that they hate being able to see the bedrooms from the main living space. Contrast provides valuable feedback for helping people make progress.

Here's another example of prototyping. I'll take my kids to a college that I know they're not going to attend, just to learn their value code. They get to experience something different, which allows them to better understand what they want. Now, suddenly, they know they want a smaller campus or an urban environment. Prototyping allows you to pick apart the pieces and understand what parts are the most desirable so you can build an ideal solution. It's about giving them distinction.

Framing the struggling moment and unpacking are all about context. Prototyping is about building contrast to create meaning. This is not about building real options. It's about showing them things that are different enough so that you can have a deeper conversation. It's fact-finding and scenario building before you've found the solution to their problem. Understanding what they don't want helps shape the design requirements.

By pulling in contrasting solutions, you understand both their tradeoffs and design requirements. We call this prototyping to learn.

4. DESIGNING TO DECIDE

You've framed the struggling moment, unpacked their words, and given them three prototypes. Now you're ready to design their progress with three possible solutions. Three's the magic number. People need to be able to eliminate options in order to decide but not too many options, which only serves to confuse.

Let's say you're selling cars. Here's where you lay out the options that meet their needs in varying ways: "I've got the Suburban, an oversized SUV, at $45,000 with 10,000 miles. It fits all your requirements, but it's larger than you wanted. I've got the Honda Odyssey, a minivan, which I know you said you didn't want, but it meets your needs exactly. It gets everybody in and out easily with remote doors, and it's a little smaller than the Suburban. It's also going to be $45,000, with 12,000 miles. Finally, I have the Kia Sorento, an SUV, the smallest of the three options, but it's loaded with everything. It's also $45,000 with 10,000 miles." Here we created three different options with different sets of tradeoffs but the same price tag. Now they'll almost immediately eliminate one, which is important. This is how you close a sale, by giving them three well-designed options that frame the tradeoffs that they're willing to make.

They've said they don't want a minivan. But they also said they like that the doors close automatically and that it fits in their garage, things the Suburban can't do. They've never had a Kia and it's smaller. So, now you've framed the tradeoffs nicely with three neat options that are different enough but meet their criteria. To be honest, nobody wants a minivan but making these tradeoffs is the way everybody ends up buying one. If we only present the minivan, people would not be able to choose. It's the tradeoffs that frame the decision.

5. PLAYING IT OUT

This is where you help the buyer see around corners and look to the future. Ask the buyer questions in advance that help them play it out; it's a test: How do you know you'll be satisfied? What are your measures of satisfaction? What are the outcomes that will make you realize you made the right purchase? It's about metrics. Without these questions there can be unintended consequences that lead to buyer's remorse.

For example, let's say you bought a new car: What are you

going to do with the old car? When do you want the new one delivered? How do you want to handle maintenance? Do you need a roof-rack on top? Let's say you bought a house: How are you going to pack up and move? Will your furniture fit in the new house? Do you need to send things to storage?

If you don't bring these things up, you can't help them understand the next sixty to ninety days. By anticipating these issues, you help them mentally prepare and prevent buyer's remorse. Playing it out involves things the buyer didn't necessarily think of. It's about setting expectations.

ABOUT THE AUTHORS

BOB MOESTA is one of the principal architects of the Jobs to be Done theory and founder of The Re-Wired Group. Since developing the Jobs to be Done theory in the mid-90s along with Harvard Business School Professor Clayton Christensen, Bob has continued to develop, advance, and apply the innovation framework to everyday business challenges.

A visual thinker, teacher, and creator, Bob has worked on and helped launch more than 3,500 new products, services, and businesses across nearly every industry, including defense, automotive, software, financial services, and education, among many others. He has started, built, and sold several startups.

Bob is an entrepreneur at heart, and engineer and designer by training. He started out as an intern for Dr. W. Edwards Deming, father of the quality revolution, and worked with Dr.

Genichi Taguchi extensively. In Japan, Bob learned firsthand many of the lean product development methods for which so many Japanese businesses, including Toyota, are known.

A lifetime learner, Bob holds degrees from Michigan State University, Harvard Business School, and Stanford University. He has studied extensively at Boston University's School of Management and at MIT School of Engineering. He is a fellow at the Clayton Christensen Institute and is a guest lecturer at the Harvard Business School, MIT Sloan School of Entrepreneurship, and Northwestern University's Kellogg School of Management.

GREG ENGLE co-founded The Re-Wired Group with Bob Moesta and Chris Spiek in 2009.

Greg's constant curiosity and extraordinary perception enable him to recognize patterns before anyone else. He is keenly observant, picking up on nuances of words, tone, and body language to quickly figure out how people work, what motivates them, and what they will do next.

Combining his perception and pattern recognition skills with an extensive sales and sales management background, Greg is a natural teacher and coach. He motivates individuals and teams utilizing everyone's strengths to pull it all together. He believes that teaching is about skills—that people have to be able to do—not just know.

ACKNOWLEDGMENTS

Writing a book is a huge undertaking that is not done alone, though there is usually only one author. This book, like my previous books, is a culmination of so many of my life experiences, collaborations, and research done with others. It is impossible for me to acknowledge everyone who has contributed to me, my life, and this book over my years. I have received so much help as a dyslexic kid from Detroit. I am thankful to so many people, too many to list everyone, but you know who you are, and I am blessed, thankful, and truly appreciate all of the help throughout the years. THANK YOU!

That said, I have a few, very specific people who helped me directly on this book.

I want to thank Greg Engle for being my business partner for almost two decades. We make a great team, and this is as much yours as it is mine. We talk through everything together.

I want to thank my family. Family is the core of everything for me, and this book would not be possible without them. To my wife Julie, for all her encouragement, and our kids Marty, Mary, Henry, and Susie, as well as my brothers Bill, Alan, and Greg as well as my sisters Sue, Jane, and Patrice, thank you for creating an environment that enabled me to write this book. To my late mom and saint, Mary, who was endlessly patient. I had way too much energy, and she channeled it in a way that enabled me to become more than a baggage handler, which were the results of my high school occupational test.

To the people who shaped my mind and influenced my thinking, wrestling with me both intellectually and tactically to solve specific problems: Dr. W. Edwards Deming, Professor Clayton Christensen, Dr. Genichi Taguchi, Yuin Wu, Yoji Akao, Dr. Don Clausing, Prof. Kim B. Clark, Jason Fried, Ryan Singer, Michael Horn, David Schonthal, Craig Wortmann, and Greg Yzerski.

To my coworkers at The Re-Wired Group, and the people who I've worked with throughout the years, especially Greg Engle, Chris Speik, Matt Sheppard, Ervin Fowlkes, Lauren Lackey, Bob Barrett, Brian Tolle, and Alan Lowenthal.

To everyone I've worked with throughout the thirty years of my adult life that have had an impact on me and selling, and therefore impacted the book, especially Bob Ericson, Mike Schrader, Gerry Weinberg, Andrew Glaser, Brian Walker,

Ethan Bernstein, Derek Van Bever, John Palmer, Rick Pedi, Chris Spiek, Kyle Bazzy, Derek Sutton, Rob Wengel, Ilya Sterin, and Neal Sales-Griffin.

I also want to thank the people who worked on this book from Scribe Media, especially Janet Murnaghan, Barbara Boyd, Emily Anderson, Rachel Brandenburg, Zach Obront, and Tucker Max. And the people who read the book in advance and offered feedback: Julie Moesta, Greg Engle, Ryan Singer, Michael Horn, Des Traynor, Bill Aulet, Paul LeBlanc, Todd Rose, John Roselli, Tim Fraser, David Schonthal, Craig Wortmann, Peter Muir, Kyle Bazzy, Derek Sutton, Mike Belsito, Paul McAvinchey, Lauren Lackey, Efosa Ojomo, Jay Gerhart, Vivian Price, Cliff Maxwell, Aaron Wetzel, Emily Snyder, and Jon Palmer.

A special thank you to Jason Fried for being a great thinking partner, collaborator, and for writing the foreword to this book.

This book is a combination of life experiences; there were so many people involved. These acknowledgements are the 20 percent that represents the 80 percent of all the people who have helped me. Thank you!

Made in the USA
Monee, IL
22 February 2021